Satisfied

A Promise of Peace in a Troubled World

Rexella Van Impe

Printed in the United States of America

Box J, Royal Oak, Michigan 48068
Box 1717, Postal Station A
Windsor, Ontario, N9A 6Y1 Canada

All Scripture quotations are from **The King James Version** of the Bible.

To my beloved father, now in the Lord's presence, and my precious mother who is a continuing inspiration in my life. Through your instruction and example, I came to know and understand the truth of satisfaction. Thank you, Dad and Mom, for this rare and rewarding privilege. I shall forever be grateful to you both.

Rexella Van Impe

CONTENTS

Foreword

Dissatisfaction is the universal malady of our age. I became more aware of this when I tuned in a local morning television program featuring an unusually articulate psychologist who spoke about coping in society. To clarify a point, the host asked the studio audience this question: "How many of you are satisfied with your life?"

As the camera panned over the group of about 150, only three hands were raised. For me, the sight of so many silently affirming that they were *not* satisfied with life was heartbreaking. As I pondered the tragedy of such reality, I realized that this studio audience was simply a microcosm of society. The problems that unsettle us in our anti-parent, anti-family, youth-bedazzled culture all reflect a general feeling of dissatisfaction. And Christians are not exempt.

It's not surprising to me that there is so much dissatisfaction among non-Christians, but to know that it exists in the lives of Christians may come as a surprise to some readers. There may be those reading this who have recognized an uneasiness in their lives, or have seen it in others they love and know, but you have struggled, too, with identifying it correctly. We don't really like to admit to being dissatisfied.

At Jack Van Impe Ministries, we receive hundreds of letters from people expressing dissatisfaction in a variety of ways. Many of them are experiencing marital problems — some of them are already separated, going through a divorce, or they are on the brink of divorce. There are letters from those who find their jobs tedious and unrewarding; others are unemployed, struggling to keep a roof over their heads and food on the table. Still others are discouraged with life in general — the state of the economy, the government, the business community. There is disillusionment over interpersonl relationships. Health problems plague many. Others feel deprived that life has somehow passed them by and all they've known is hardship. A vast number of letters tug at the heart as mothers and fathers cry out their disappointment about their children — many of these are married children needing help just at the time their parents feel they are finally entitled to enjoy their retirement years. The majority of these people want advice and help. They ask us to pray that their lives will become better. All of them, I sense, are seeking lasting satisfaction.

As my husband and I have traveled across America and in foreign lands, God has allowed us the privilege of ministering to more than ten million people face-to-face. The trials, sorrows, doubts, and fears that many of them shared with us have, in a large measure, prompted me to write this book because wherever we have traveled and to whomever we have ministered, we have consistently discovered two indisputable truths. The first is that these individuals are not alone. No matter how difficult their situation or how deep the burden they bear, others either have or are experiencing something very similar. The second reality is that their lives can be transformed through the miracle-working power of God and an unqualified surrender to His will.

There is a sense in which some dissatisfaction is necessary in our lives; I'll be talking about that, too. There will be those who say what this book has to offer is "simplistic advice." The apostle Paul had something to say about this: *For the preaching of the cross is to them that perish foolishness; but unto us which are saved it is the power of God . . . Because the foolishness of God is wiser than men; and the weakness of God is stronger than men . . . But God hath chosen the foolish things of the world to confound the wise; and God hath chosen the weak things of the world to confound the things which are mighty* (I Corinthians 1:18, 25, 27).

There are many paths the world follows in its vain pursuit of satisfaction, but sooner or later people discover that much of what they have been seeking does not provide lasting satisfaction. There must be something more.

What is that "something more"?

It is my prayer that, as you read this book, you will be drawn to the abundant, satisfying life God has promised to those who stay close to Him.

Section I

Dissatisfied and Searching: Why?

I Am Fearfully and Wonderfully Made

I'll never forget meeting Phyllis.

We were at a college in Chattanooga, Tennessee, conducting a series of meetings with the student body. When I sing, I endeavor to establish eye contact with people in the audience, and as I looked over that large group of students, my eyes met hers. She was right in the front, looking up with an angelic face, totally absorbed in the words of my song. I could hardly take my eyes off her.

Phyllis had obviously been born with a defect that hindered her growth. Though she was an adult, she was the size of an infant. Her little legs were too small to enable her to walk well, so she got around by means of a small child's tricycle. She looked like a tiny doll, sitting on her trike, quietly listening to my song. I don't think I've ever felt such an instant, deep love for anyone as I felt for Phyllis that day.

When the service concluded, Phyllis asked a friend to bring me to her. Without any hesitation, I did what I had been longing to do from the moment I first saw her. I took her in my arms and hugged her.

Psalm 139:14 says, *I will praise thee; for I am fearfully and wonderfully made: marvelous are thy works; and that my soul knoweth right well.* As I talked with Phyllis this verse came to mind, and I was struck by the thought that the truth of this psalm applied to her just as surely as it applied to the psalmist, or to me, or to anyone else! God *had* fashioned Phyllis, and regardless of her appearance from our human perspective, He had not made a mistake.

I was particularly impressed by the depth of Phyllis' quiet beauty. From what I could tell in that brief encounter, she had no self-image problems. To the contrary, she appeared confident, strong, and spiritually mature. As she shared the concerns of her heart with me so that I might pray with her, I noticed that not one of her requests was selfish. Phyllis asked me to pray for her roommates, for her loved ones, and about some problems she was aware of involving other students. She did not ask me to pray for her. Although her physical problems and the difficulties she had getting around resulted in very pressing personal needs, the focus of her concern was on the needs of others.

Phyllis had grasped a truth that most people completely miss: that we are created by God for His glory. Consequently, she was content with the way she was. She was fearfully and wonderfully made, and for someone of such small stature, she had touched a multitude of lives.

A Designer Original

In our society, self-acceptance is a rare reality. Although people today tend to spend a good deal of time thinking about themselves — ours may just be the most self-centered generation ever — most people simply do not like themselves. Such self-rejection is completely debilitating, for the one who is dissatisfied with himself has a more difficult time finding true satisfaction.

I believe Psalm 139 was written for those whose dissatisfaction is focused on themselves. Three truths in this psalm provide for the development of an individual sense of self-worth. First of all, *God made us.* Verse 16 states: *...in thy book all my members were written...when as yet there was none of them.* Thus, we see that God has not only made us, but He has made us according to a perfect plan. We are not accidents. Instead, as a special creation each of us has intrinsic value. Regardless of our physical condition, appearance, or abilities, we are of great value to God, for we were made to glorify Him.

Mary Crowley, president of Home Interiors and Gifts, Inc., of Dallas, Texas — a very successful businesswoman — has as a motto, "Be somebody — God doesn't take time to make a nobody." Mary, by giving unselfishly of herself, has earned the respect of the business and political world. She told me in an interview that she feels God has gifted her with the ability to motivate others. She works with the women she employs, helping them to build a strong self-image, with an emphasis on developing inner qualities of beauty. "My self-image is tied up in the character of God himself," she said. "I want every woman to know that inside her, God has created the potential of genius."

Contemporary humanity is obsessed with outward appearances. We tend to think that if something looks good it *is* good, and if it doesn't look good, it isn't. As a result, our focus is on externals — clothing, weight, the way we style our hair, and the way we make up our faces. I do not mean to imply that these things are not important; they are (and I will be sharing more about one's personal appearance in chapter 8). Looking good can make you feel better about yourself, and you may even act better because of it; but what I am saying is that the *emphasis* too often is out of balance. The way we look must always take second place to the condition of the spirit. Mary Kay Ash, founder and president of one of America's most successful cosmetic companies, says, "True beauty comes from within. You have to feel good about yourself."

The Myths of the Advertising World

The advertising world constantly feeds our obsession about our looks with television commercials appealing to our inner cravings to be beautiful and accepted. They tell us diet soft drinks will ensure a slim body; that by using the right toothpaste we will have sparkling teeth; and that a certain brand of shampoo will take care of our dandruff problems — people will reject you if they catch you scratching an itchy scalp. And on and on it goes.

Any thinking person should recognize that this is

nonsense, but we are lured by promises into buying the products. One can be slim, beautiful, and young looking and still not be satisfied. The incidence of suicide among young models and movie stars is proof that externals do not satisfy.

Furthermore, putting sizzle into a relationship with exotic perfumes and by dressing seductively is no guarantee of long-lasting satisfaction. The assault by the media upon our senses with images of gorgeous women and macho men who give every appearance of having attained the ultimate in satisfaction is a myth.

The list of gifted, creative, and attractive people who have killed themselves is long. These were people who had achieved it to the top of the ladder. Supposedly, they were successful and satisfied. Any such list is tragic. You may recognize some of these names: John Berryman, Anne Sexton, Hart Crane, Virginia Woolf, Sylvia Plath, Ernest Hemingway, Marilyn Monroe, Vincent Van Gogh, Thomas Chatterton, and even Socrates. So it can be seen that unless a person has come to terms with himself, with his uniqueness as one of God's children, no amount of money, fame, or effort expended on ways to change one's self-image is going to bring durable satisfaction.

The result of modern marketing's emphasis on the external, the visible, is simply more self-rejection. Commercials are *designed* to make us dissatisfied with the way we are. Their aim, of course, is getting us to want their products. We are actually being brainwashed into a wrong perspective. We are being programmed to be dissatisfied with ourselves. We are being taught to focus on the externals only. Consequently, many totally neglect the fundamental truths that God made us to reflect His glory and that how we look on the outside is of fleeting importance.

Looks change. Of all our temporal possessions, outward appearance is perhaps the one that fades first. It can be destroyed instantly by an accident, or it slowly deteriorates. No one stays young forever, and everyone who lives long enough will have wrinkles, a change in the color and texture of their hair or even baldness, and show other signs of aging.

On the other hand, God's workmanship in us involves qualities of character He desires to build into our lives. For example, He wants us to be reflections of His love. He also desires that we exhibit integrity, purity, and holiness. He wants us to be patient, kind, and humble. *None of these things can be accomplished by altering the way we look!*

On one of our television programs, I had the delightful privilege of interviewing Dee Jepson, wife of Senator Roger Jepson of Iowa. (She also served as Special Assistant to the President for Public Liaison during the Reagan administration.)

Dee told me that a turning point in her life came when she realized that her career, her status in life, and her material successes were not what gave her life meaning. She saw that because she was a creation of a good and almighty and loving God, she had value as a person that would be there even if her career came suddenly to an end or if she lost every material possession. She said:

> In a day and age when women are seeking their identity, I think that oftentimes they are

> looking in the wrong places. I think it is very important that they realize that we need to find our identity in our importance as human beings just because we are. I think it is very important that we find our value and our identity in the fact that we are children of a creative God.
>
> I also feel that women need to realize that as they make their choices in life, if they choose to be a homemaker and stay home and contribute in that way, that is an immensely important role. If they serve their family, support their husband's career, make a house a home, shape and mold young lives, they are making a major contribution to society. They shouldn't feel any guilt or societal pressures to go out and make some kind of mark in the marketplace.

Dee is one of those people who exudes confidence and strength and security. Her secret is that she does not base her sense of self-worth on anything that can be taken away from her. Her confidence comes from the fact that she knows the One who made her. She knows He loves her, and thus she can accept herself. As she puts it, "For me, Jesus Christ is the center of my life, and that is what life is all about. If you are attempting to be, and willing to be, in the center of His will, it makes things so much easier because it sort of transfers the responsibility to Him." This kind of attitude and understanding builds the kind of satisfaction that nothing external can ever take away.

Cooperating With the Designer

A second truth from Psalm 139 is that *God knows*

us. In fact, He knows everything that can be known about us. He knows us better than we know ourselves. The psalmist wrote:

O Lord, thou hast searched me, and known me. Thou knowest my downsitting and mine uprising, thou understandest my thought afar off. Thou compassest my path and my lying down, and art acquainted with all my ways. For there is not a word in my tongue, but, lo, O Lord, thou knowest it altogether. Thou hast beset me behind and before, and laid thine hand upon me. Such knowledge is too wonderful for me; it is high, I cannot attain unto it (verses 1-6).

One reason we, as human beings, are so concerned with externals is that much of what we can see of others is what shows from the outside. God, however, is not so limited: *...the Lord seeth not as man seeth; for man looketh on the outward appearance, but the Lord looketh on the heart* (I Samuel 16:7). Yes, God knows everything about us! He can see behind the exterior, behind our disguises, masks, and facades. He knows what is in our hearts. He knows what is in our minds. He even knows the words that are in our mouths before we speak. And yet He loves us!

Not everyone is comforted by this fact, and that is certainly understandable. If God knows all the secrets of our hearts, all our thoughts, all our desires, and all our feelings, He knows some horrible things, doesn't He? In addition, if we understand that God is holy and hates sin, the fact that He knows everything about us can become even more frightening, for all of us are guilty of sin. We cannot keep the deepest secrets of our hearts hidden from God; He knows them.

Nevertheless, despite our secret sins, God reaches out to us in love. The corruption of our hearts does not change His compassion and care for us. The wonderful truth is that He offers His forgiveness, continuing love, and salvation unconditionally to all those who will trust Him. He *could* deal with us as enemies, but He chooses to love us.

Please don't misunderstand me. I do not believe that self-acceptance is the same as self-indulgence. True self-acceptance does not mean that we abandon ourselves to our faults or that we blind ourselves to our character flaws. Rather, it means that we recognize them for what they are — sin — confess them, and determine to cooperate with God's work in conforming us to His image. Does that sound difficult? Then remember Dee Jepson's statement that when we do this the responsibility transfers to God. Second Corinthians 5:17 states: *Therefore if any man be in Christ, he is a new creature* [or creation]: *old things are passed away; behold, all things are become new.* What a blessed truth. We *can* be like the Lord because of His work within us!

Companionship That Satisfies

A final truth from Psalm 139 is that *God is with us.*

Whither shall I go from thy spirit? or whither shall I flee from thy presence? If I ascend up into heaven, thou art there: if I make my bed in hell, behold, thou art there. If I take the wings of the morning, and dwell in the uttermost parts of the sea; Even there shall thy hand lead me, and thy right hand shall hold me. If I say, Surely the darkness shall cover me; even the night shall be light about me. Yea, the darkness hideth not from thee; but the night shineth as the day: the darkness and the light are both alike to thee (verses 7-12).

How marvelous to know that God, having made us, did not simply abandon us to ourselves! What assurance there is in knowing that He didn't just create the universe, set things in motion, and then walk off and leave it to whatever fate lay ahead! God *wants* to be with us, fellowship with us, commune with us, know us, and have us know Him intimately. This, apart from anything else we say or do or become, gives each of us tremendous value.

Nothing gives me more confidence than the knowledge that God is with me. I could not sing before thousands, travel as I do, or appear in front of a television camera for a nationwide program without the knowledge that God is with me and that He has called me and is empowering me to do what I am doing.

Each of us, you see, is a bit like Moses, who had a definite self-image problem. Perhaps he had it because his first attempt to lead the Israelites ended in incredible failure: he killed a man, was publicly humiliated, had to give up his position of status and wealth, and spent 40 years on the back side of the desert thinking about it. How miserable he must have been. Then God appeared to him in a burning bush and called him to confront Pharaoh on behalf of the children of Israel.

Moses, his ego wounded from his previous failure, didn't think he had what it would take to speak for the

Lord. He protested, *I am slow of speech, and of a slow tongue* (Exodus 4:10). God answered him, *I will be with thy mouth, and teach thee what thou shalt say* (verse 12). What an incentive to service that was! God himself promised not only to be with Moses but to give him guidance and instruction as well. He promises the same to you and me.

Yes, the God who made us and knows all about us wants us to know Him in His fullness. That is why He has revealed himself through His Word. He wants us to walk with Him, to enjoy His presence, to draw on His strength, and to lean on Him in times of uncertainty and pain. His promise is, *I will never leave thee, nor forsake thee* (Hebrews 13:5).

In the early days of our ministry, there were times when I was very sick. I can remember getting out of bed to sing in meetings and then, later, returning to bed with heavy medication. Sometimes the pain was so excruciating I did not feel I could sing another note. Yet, when I was weak, the Lord sustained me. When I was tired, He strengthened me. When I hurt, He comforted me. I could never have done it in my own strength. Through those experiences, I learned the same truths Paul discovered during his ministry: God's grace *is* sufficient. His strength is most powerful in the midst of our weaknesses (see II Corinthians 12:9).

Most of all, I learned that God made me the way He did for a purpose. If I had been given the opportunity to choose my characteristics as an evangelist's wife, I probably would have asked for a tremendous amount of stamina and physical strength. I would have requested perfect health and unlimited abilities.

God, in His infinite wisdom, did not make me that way. Instead, He has used my weaknesses to amplify *His* strength, and I can say without reservation that I am completely satisfied with the way He has made me. Praise to Him alone, in the more than 30 years that I have labored with my husband in the ministry, I have missed only eight weeks of meetings, and that was due to major surgery. Perhaps even a robust person could not do this except by God's grace.

My heart aches for those who are not satisfied with themselves. I wish they knew the satisfaction of resting in the confidence that God made us, He knows everything about us, and He is with us. Ultimately, you see, the person who rejects himself is really rejecting the God who made him the way he is. For such a person, there is no hope of true satisfaction.

Count It All Joy

There is no easy road to satisfaction. One reason for this is that no one has ever lived a life free from difficulties. Everyone faces trials, and all of us know suffering in one way or another. I've noticed that wherever I am, in every culture and every geographical region, when I mention the subject of suffering, there is an instant rapport, a bond of mutual understanding.

Suffering: A Door to Finding Satisfaction

We can take comfort in the knowledge that Scripture teaches that God's perfect plan for each of us includes suffering, trials, and pain. The wonderful truth is that our most frustrating trials can be a source of great joy. James wrote:

My brethren, count it all joy when ye fall into

divers temptations; Knowing this, that the trying of your faith worketh patience. But let patience have her perfect work, that ye may be perfect and entire, wanting nothing (James 1:2-4). Trials will make us either bitter or better.

I know what it is like to be broken — literally. In my book *The Tender Touch*, I told of the terrible automobile accident my husband and I experienced in Brussels in 1979. We were in Europe for our twenty-seventh wedding anniversary and planned to celebrate the joyous occasion with members of Jack's family.

That particular afternoon, we had traveled to Brussels to shop for anniversary gifts. We leisurely walked and talked, truly enjoying our visit to this fascinating city. We even stopped for afternoon tea and shared a sandwich. (A cousin was preparing a feast for our anniversary dinner that night and we didn't want to ruin our appetites!)

The afternoon ended all too quickly, and we soon found ourselves driving back to the home of the cousin with whom we were staying. Suddenly, seemingly out of nowhere, a bus traveling 50 miles an hour struck our vehicle with such impact that my side of the car was ripped away and the rest of the automobile completely demolished. I remember saying, "Jack, there's a bus!" He attempted to swerve, but it was too late. My last thought as I fell out onto the busy street was, *This is what it's like to die.*

Everything went black. I felt no pain until my husband's warm tears falling on my face revived me. His voice was choked with emotion as he wept and prayed over me, "Lord, must it end this way? Don't let it happen. Please work a miracle!"

I felt that I was slipping away from him, and I wanted him to know how much I loved him. "Honey, I think I am dying," I whispered. "I don't want to leave you."

"Oh, no," Jack cried. "Oh, God, please help us. Somehow spare her life."

I wish that in some way I could convey the peace that I experienced from God during this time. Even Christians sometimes wonder about and perhaps are somewhat afraid of the unknown — that valley of the shadow of death through which we must one day pass. I would love to stand on a mountaintop and call to every believer everywhere, "Don't be afraid!" At the moment of departure, He is there to give us peace and sustain our hearts. What a comfort to know that we are the Lord's most prized possessions and that He will never allow us to go through the transition from this world to the next in fear. I rejoice over this experience today because I can say with David, *I will fear no evil; for thou art with me* (Psalm 23:4).

Suspended in God's sweet peace, I was almost in the presence of the Lord. Then suddenly, I was pulled back from going over. A hand grasped my wrist and a man stood beside me. He tenderly placed a blanket over my body and in perfect English said, "Don't move her. She will be all right." Immediately, my mind began to clear and I knew that I would live.

As quickly as he had appeared, he was gone. The Lord had sent a man or an angel (only He knows) to provide perfect comfort and to minister to us in a special way. Hebrews 1:14 says: *Are they* [angels] *not all ministering spirits, sent forth to minister for them who shall be heirs of salvation?*

An ambulance rushed us to the hospital. I looked at Jack and was reassured to know that he was all right. I knew that somehow God was doing something special in our lives — something that would ultimately glorify Him if we would not faint (see II Corinthians 4:16).

I had sustained a severe head injury. X rays revealed that I had a broken collarbone and two broken ribs. I had also sustained numerous cuts and bruises, and fragments of glass were embedded in parts of my body. In fact, the doctor spent four hours removing glass from my legs, head, and ears. God had divinely and miraculously spared my face and eyes, for which I shall forever be grateful.

Because of my head injury, I was unable to receive any pain medication for 18 hours. In addition, I was told that if the bleeding from my head wound did not stop during the night, doctors would be forced to shave my head in order to suture the extreme abrasion. Jack remained by my side every minute of that entire night, praying with me, comforting me, and talking with me. We asked God for a miracle, and He gave us one. By morning, the bleeding had stopped.

Neither of us slept during that long, unforgettable night. As we talked about *why* it happened, I felt a kinship with Job. God had allowed Satan to test us but not destroy us or our ministry together. He allowed the test to go so far, and no further. I knew that my Father was in control and that my Saviour was not leaving me alone. Indeed, I knew that He was feeling my infirmity with even greater intensity than I.

Jack spent the next 48 hours trying to get the doctors to release me for our return to America.

British Airways agreed to fly us and graciously provided wheelchair and ambulance service all the way to Detroit. Still, the hours in flight were painfully long, *Notwithstanding the Lord stood with me, and strengthened me* (II Timothy 4:17).

During the next three months, I received extensive medical treatment and stringent therapy. Adhesions formed as the damaged muscles and tendons in my crushed shoulder healed. Doctors said that without corrective surgery I would never use my arm again. Instead, I underwent months of excruciating rehabilitative exercises to correct the situation. Still, I would not want to look back upon this experience with anything but rejoicing and praise — rejoicing in the Lord's protection and love in bringing me through this trial and praise that He counted me worthy to be put to the test.

Resistance to Suffering is Counterproductive

It would have been easy, I suppose, to *resist* in my heart and be bitter against the Lord for allowing such a thing to happen. Yet it never occurred to me to question what God was doing. Years earlier Jack and I had committed ourselves to pursuing the Lord's will whatever the cost — and when we made that commitment, we knew it could involve suffering. It has, but the rewards have been rich. God has filled our lives with blessings that exceed anything we could ask or think.

Unfortunately, instead of counting problems and trials as joy and allowing them to work patience and maturity, many people tend to follow their natural inclination, and the difficulties produce bitterness and resentment. That, in turn, only amplifies dissatisfaction, until finally they are caught in a never-ending cycle of devastatingly negative feelings.

The only effect resistance has on our trials is to make them more difficult to bear. When we rebel against God and turn from Him, we shut out the One who can enable us to carry whatever burden He gives us. How tragic it is to see someone who has gone through grief and pain who then turns sorrow into bitterness against God! That is not what God wants. He wants to make the burden light and the yoke easy to bear (see Matthew 11:30).

I know that it is normal to want to resist problems, and, of course, it is right and even necessary to resist some things. For example, we should not give in to immoral acts, so we must resist temptation. Scripture tells us to resist Satan (see James 4:7; I Peter 5:9). Nevertheless, when we are confronted with trials that are beyond our control, we need to see ourselves as Paul did — like clay in the hands of the Potter, submissive to His will for our lives. We must realize that through these trials He is molding us, shaping us, and perfecting us — until we become vessels that He can use.

Have you ever watched a potter work on a pottery wheel? He squeezes and pinches and applies pressure, and from what was an ugly lump of clay comes forth a beautiful, useful piece of pottery. The potter knows just where to poke and just where to rub — it is a fascinating process to watch. Occasionally, the potter will decide a radical change is in order, and he will smash a nearly molded pot and begin again from the beginning.

Jeremiah described the process:

I went down to the potter's house, and, behold, he wrought a work on the wheels. And the vessel that he made of clay was marred in the hand of the potter: so he made it again another vessel, as seemed good to the potter to make it (Jeremiah 18:3-4).

Perhaps you feel like the Potter has smashed you that way. I have good news for you. God is one Potter who always rebuilds the vessels He allows to be broken so that they are better than before. It may not always be in the way we desire or think is best, but in the process, it is nonproductive for us to resist and become bitter. Instead we should try to see what is happening from God's perspective, even though we may not understand what He is doing, and yield to His will for us. Paul wrote, *Shall the thing formed say to him that formed it, Why hast thou made me thus? Hath not the potter power over the clay?* (Romans 9:20, 21).

Acceptance: A New Name for Satisfaction

How much better it is to *accept* our trials as from the Lord who permits them! Job accepted his trials, as hard as they were for him. This incredible man lost all his earthly possessions and all his children in a series of disasters that happened in just one day. Soon after that, he lost his health as well. He was reduced to a mass of sores, sitting in a pile of ashes, scraping himself with a piece of broken pottery (how appropriate!). He did not understand what God was doing, but his response was, *The Lord gave, and the Lord hath taken away; blessed be the name of the Lord . . . Shall we receive good at the hand of God, and shall we not receive evil?* (Job 1:21; 2:10).

Yes, Job bore all the pain — in his case both physical pain and mental anguish — and did not sin with his lips. He never accused God or spoke bitterly against Him. Quite the contrary, Job accepted the negative things as graciously as he had accepted the good things. Though the task was not easy, out of Job's afflictions came some wonderful fruit. The first is the book of Job — a rich source of comfort in times of despair and doubt. In addition, Job grew wiser and closer to the Lord through his ordeal. Even his so-called comforters learned from his sufferings.

What became of Job? The answer is recorded for us in verses 12 and 16 of chapter 42: *So the Lord blessed the latter end of Job more than his beginning. After this lived Job an hundred and forty years . . .*

The "secret" of Job's success and blessing is rooted in the fact that he *endured* his suffering. He never turned from God. Instead, he repented! Why would a man who was *perfect and upright, and one that feared God, and eschewed evil* (1:1) do such a thing? Because Job, through his suffering, was privileged to get a glimpse of God in His holiness. As a result, he saw himself as so completely unworthy that he said, *I abhor myself* (42:6). And in doing that, he discovered yet a third way of responding to trials.

Rejoicing: A Perspective You May Have Overlooked

This third type of response is what James referred

to in the opening passage of this chapter — *rejoicing*, or glorying, in our trials. Admittedly, rejoicing in the midst of tribulation is not an easy thing to do. A woman wrote to us a short time ago:

> I am having a very hard time adjusting my life. My husband died not too long ago at age 53, and I just can't seem to get my life together. I never worked in all the years we were married. I was a family person and never made many friends outside our home. I am lonely and frightened. Please pray for me.

My heart goes out to this dear woman and many others like her. In fact, one might well ask how she could possibly rejoice in the midst of such a difficult trial. She cannot rejoice that her husband has died. How then can she find joy in the midst of her deep loneliness, fear, and doubts?

The answer is found in the perspective we choose to take. No one rejoices in the death of a loved one. Job didn't, and even Jesus wept at the grave of His friend Lazarus. Scripture acknowledges that sorrow and grief are appropriate and normal responses to death.

Bitterness comes when we focus on our sorrows or trials themselves rather than on the Lord and what He is attempting to accomplish through them. From this perspective, we can easily become discouraged. Unfortunately, this is exactly the place in which many dissatisfied people find themselves. However, if we look beyond the trials and understand that God is working in the midst of them, if we focus our hearts on Him, a miracle begins to occur. He brings peace in the midst of pain, and joy in the midst of sorrow. Truly, His grace *is* sufficient.

My Grandmother Shelton taught me firsthand the meaning of glorying in tribulation. She knew trials all her life. She was the mother of eight children and, as a diabetic, had to take insulin shots every day of her life. She was a tall, vibrant, robust lady who would pick me up (literally) and shake me like a rag doll and say, "I love you, Rexella." What a shock when she lost first one leg, then the other, to amputation because of complications from her disease. She would never walk again; yet, I never heard her mention her trials or complain. Her focus went far beyond them. And as she looked to the Lord and leaned on Him, she was actually able to glory in her infirmities! She was always rejoicing. I remember her often taking out a little harmonica and playing it. Just being around her brought me great joy, and I seldom thought of her as being in pain, although I'm certain she suffered greatly.

There is something to be said for pain. Trials are not pleasant, but they are valuable. A flower must be crushed before it yields perfume. A grain of wheat must fall to the ground and die before it can bear fruit (see John 12:24). And we must suffer for the Lord if we are to be glorified with Him (see Romans 8:17).

If you are going through a trial, don't resist it. And don't just accept it or endure it. Learn to glory in it! God is doing something through your trials. You may not understand it fully, and He does not always give us explanations. But He does give us promises — and He always keeps them.

> *Trials are medicines which our gracious and wise physician prescribes, because we need them; and he proportions the frequency and weight of them to what the case requires. Let us trust his skill and thank him for his prescription.*
>
> —*Isaac Newton*

I came across something that helped me to further understand these precious truths. In Job 41:25 are to be found these few obscure words: *By reason of breakings they purify themselves.* What can that possibly mean?

Elsewhere the Bible teaches that the sacrifices God accepts are broken and contrite hearts (see Psalm 51:17). This is illustrated throughout the Bible as one observes God using for His glory those people and things which are most perfectly broken. Here are some examples:

> Jacob at Peniel, where his natural strength was broken.

> Moses and the rock at Horeb; when he struck it, out gushed cool water for the thirsty people.

> Gideon and his band of 300 elect soldiers. When they broke their pitchers — a type of breaking of themselves — their hidden lights shone forth to the consternation of their adversaries.

The poor widow who broke the seal on the little pot of oil, and it poured forth, whereby God multiplied it to pay her debts and her sons didn't have to be taken as bondmen.

Queen Esther risking her life, breaking through the rigid etiquette of a heathen court, thus obtaining favor to rescue her people from death.

Jesus taking the five loaves of bread, breaking them, and in the act of breaking, there was sufficient to feed 5,000.

Mary breaking her alabaster box, rendering it useless, but this allowed the perfume to fill the house.

Jesus allowing His body to be broken by thorns, nails, and the spear, so that His life was poured out for us to live.

God must have broken things — throughout all plant life, all history, all the great biographical accounts, and in all spiritual life, this fact is preeminent.

Why should we then shrink from those things which may break us at some point? If we will but allow Him, the brokenness we experience can be used for our greater good and for God's glory. Such brokenness may come in the form of being broken in wealth, self-will, ambitions, ideals, reputation, affections, and even brokenness in health. Remember, the final tally of life is not seen in the here and now. Can you, like James wrote, "Count it all joy?"

Footprints

One night a man had a dream. He dreamed he was walking along the beach with the LORD. Across the sky flashed scenes from his life. For each scene, he noticed two sets of footprints in the sand; one belonging to him and the other to the LORD.

When the last scene of his life flashed before him, he looked back at the footprints in the sand. He noticed that many times along the path of his life there was only one set of footprints. He also noticed that it happened at the very lowest and saddest times in his life.

This really bothered him, and he questioned the LORD about it. "LORD, You said that once I decided to follow You, You'd walk with me all the way. But I have noticed that during the most troublesome times in my life, there is only one set of footprints. I don't understand why when I needed You most You would leave me."

The LORD replied, "My precious, precious child, I love you and I would never leave you. During your times of trial and suffering, when you see only one set of footprints, it was then that I carried you."

Author unknown

Section II

The Lure of the Empty Promise: Fruitless Paths

The Myths of Our Age

We are living in an age unlike any in the history of mankind. This century alone has seen more scientific and technological advancement than all the rest of history combined. Today we take for granted things that were but science fiction just a decade ago. Yet despite all this — perhaps *because* of it — our society as a whole may be more dissatisfied than ever before.

When asked what it would take to satisfy them, most people respond with a list of things. Money, luxury items, cars, vacations, entertainment — these are what come to mind first when contemporary man thinks of being satisfied. How far from true satisfaction we have strayed!

The Myth of Instant Gratification

One fallacy that has worked its way firmly into the

fabric of modern reasoning is the belief that we can be most satisfied when the gratification of our needs and desires is immediate. I call this *the myth of instant gratification.* We have become conditioned to expect on-the-spot results from everything. There is instant coffee, instant milk, instant potatoes, instant rice, instant printing, and instant photography. If one doesn't have a camera that takes instant snapshots, he can take his film to a place that will develop it and make color prints in less than an hour! Even banks have 24-hour electronic tellers so that we don't have to wait until the facility opens. And we can even send packages across the country through a number of overnight delivery services.

There is nothing inherently wrong with any of these things. In fact, I gladly use such services and am thankful that they are available when I need them. But overnight delivery and 24-hour tellers are the mild side of our obsession with getting things we want without having to wait. It also has an ugly side.

We cringe and are grieved at the growing phenomenon of drug abuse throughout all levels of society, as people look for a pill or an injection or some kind of stimulant that will instantly make them feel good. Yet, we often fail to see the connection between this kind of behavior and the elusive promise of instant satisfaction that beckons to us along every avenue of life.

We shake our heads in dismay when we read of a con man who defrauds needy people out of thousands of dollars in some kind of get-rich-quick scheme. But isn't the greed of both the con man and his victims really just an extension of the mentality that causes people to put themselves into unmanageable debt because they want something now and do not wish to wait for it? Yes, we all must come to the realization that our pursuit of instant gratification is destroying our society like a cancer.

Luke 15 relates the familiar story of the Prodigal Son, who, like so many today, wanted instant wealth. Anxious to "do his own thing" and experience life for himself, he refused to wait for that which would be his in due time. He wanted what was coming to him *now.*

His father gave him his inheritance, and the young man immediately began squandering it in a mad pursuit of instant gratification. He traveled abroad and became caught up in the "action" of his day. "Eat, drink, and be merry," he thought, "for tomorrow we die." This humanistic philosophy of the ages quickly became his mind-set and the motivating force in his life.

Then the bottom fell out of everything. An economic crisis struck the land, and he suddenly found himself far from home. Dejected and dissatisfied, he was forced to accept the most menial of tasks just to exist, and his heart longed for what he once had and took for granted — the love and security of his father's home. As he thought on his foolish selfishness and wrongdoing, he made the most important decision of his life: *I will arise and go to my father, and will say unto him, Father, I have sinned against heaven, and before thee, And am no more worthy to be called thy son: make me as one of thy hired servants* (verses 18, 19).

Modern man is not different from that young man, except that instead of coming to his senses, acknowledging his misdeeds, and turning from them, he continues blindly onward in his pursuit of immediate gratification. He never seems to learn that the kind of gratification that is instant is generally also fleeting and seldom truly satisfying.

The Myth of Materialism

We have become hypnotized by *the myth of materialism* — the belief that material things are the source of true satisfaction. However, this is an empty and dehumanizing philosophy in which things become more important than people, beauty more desired than virtue, power more respected than character, and status more prestigious than integrity Consequently, we find ourselves foolishly pursuing the very things that God has said make closeness to Him difficult and sometimes impossible.

Although most of us do enjoy some added pleasures to our lives above and beyond our basic needs, we must ask ourselves one important question: Do they control us? As *Detroit News* staff writer Chuck Bennett states: "Let's be honest — we all love material things. At least most of us do, even if we can only dream about having them. And it seems once we begin to get a taste of them, even with one little item, we want more. Yesterday's luxury becomes today's frill and tomorrow's necessity; no matter what level we're at, we want something better."

Mr. Bennett has captured the essence of man's obsession with the material. The main problem is obvious: we never seem to have enough. When a person becomes a millionaire, he soon finds himself wanting to become a billionaire. On a lesser level, others have their hearts set on obtaining larger houses, finer automobiles, additional income, more power, and more prestige. Instead of rejoicing and being thankful for that which God has given them or allowed them to accomplish, they become consumed with a desire for still more and believe that they need it to be happy. The result is bondage.

Have you heard of the Quaker who wanted to teach a great lesson to his friends and neighbors? He had a large sign printed and put up on the vacant lot next to his house. The sign displayed these words: "I will give the deed to this lot to anyone who is absolutely contented." Applicants were directed to apply next door at his home.

There was a man of great wealth living in his community, and as he drove by and saw the sign, he stopped. He thought to himself, "If there is anyone in our area who is absolutely contented, it is I. I have everything that I could possibly want." So he went to the Quaker's house and knocked on the door.

The Quaker came to the door, and the man said, "I read the sign placed on the vacant lot next door. I understand you want to give it to anyone who is contented."

"Yes," said the Quaker.

"I think I am absolutely contented," the man replied. "I will be glad if you will make the deed out to me."

"Friend, if thee is contented, what does thee want with my lot?" the Quaker asked.

The Jewish Talmud says that man is born with his hands clenched, but he dies with his hands wide open.

How tragically empty are riches and possessions! Perhaps you have had the experience of wanting something for a long time. Maybe it was a car or a house or something less — but you desired to have it so much that it was all about which you could think. You saved for it, planned for it, hoped for it, and dreamed about it. But when you finally got it, after a time you found it to be disappointingly unfulfilling.

On the other hand, some have fallen prey to the notion that self-deprivation is the quickest and easiest path to spirituality. Such reasoning is equally fallacious and can result in a lifetime of despair and dissatisfaction.

A few years ago, during a crusade we were conducting in Atlanta, a young girl came and asked me to make an announcement concerning a local Christian ministry for runaway young people. She wanted me to tell any such persons who might be present that they would be welcome to seek help from her group. Wanting to find out more about this ministry, I asked her, "What do you do with the runaways who come to you seeking help?"

"Well," she said, "we just come together and stay and have fellowship."

"How do you get food?" I asked. "How do you support your ministry?"

"We just ask God for it," she replied.

"You mean you don't work?"

"No," she answered, amazed that I would ask such a question. "We just live there."

Further investigation revealed that the "ministry" she wanted me to promote was a communal group who went out to shopping centers and street corners and stopped people to ask them for money. Members of the group were not encouraged to seek employment or return home, nor were they learning anything of value as far as I could tell. In fact, their life-style was characterized more by slothfulness than by anything else. I lovingly explained to my youthful inquirer that the Bible teaches, *...if any would not work, neither should he eat* (II Thessalonians 3:10). God has promised to meet our needs, but He has also commanded us to be diligent, hard-working, and wise in our stewardship. There is nothing holy about begging.

Those who center their thoughts on the temporal, as well as those who refuse to acknowledge that material possessions should occupy a place in one's life, cannot be truly satisfied. And neither group is truly wealthy, no matter how much or how little money they have.

Scripture is consistent in its teaching that *the love of money is the root of all evil* (I Timothy 6:10). However, this passage is often misquoted and misapplied. Please notice that it does *not* say that *money* is the root of all evil. Rather, it is the *love* of money — the placing of material gain above the more important things in life — that brings the piercing of oneself through with many sorrows. God can, and often does, reward our faithfulness to Him and His service with material blessings.

Upon his appointment as King of Israel, Solomon asked God for *an understanding heart to judge thy people, that I may discern between good and bad* (I Kings 3:9). Because he sought the Lord and others before himself, God not only granted Solomon's request but also added, *I have also given thee that which thou hast not asked, both riches, and honor* (v. 13). Likewise, Job, whose life and trials we looked at in chapter 2, remained faithful to God, and . . . *the Lord blessed the latter end of Job more than his beginning* (Job 42:12).

Certainly, *Godliness with contentment is great gain* (I Timothy 6:6), and as we have clearly seen, it is not how much one possesses that makes him great in God's eyes and satisfied in life. To the contrary, it is whether or not he allows his possessions to possess him! Those who are truly wealthy are those who have discovered the spiritual riches and deep satisfaction that comes through a life of surrender to God.

The Myth of Prestige

In an earlier chapter we talked about the myth of success. This pursuit of prestige usually is a dead-end street in terms of lasting satisfaction. But you see it on almost every hand — in social groups, in politics, on the job, and even in the church.

What is success? To *succeed* implies the favorable outcome of an undertaking, career, etc., or the attainment of a desired goal (to *succeed* as a businessman or businesswoman). Success is the gaining of wealth, fame, rank, etc.[1] *Prestige* is the power to command admiration or esteem; or reputation or distinction based on brilliance of achievement, character, etc.; renown.[2]

Don't get me wrong; I'm not implying that it's wrong to *want* to be successful. What needs emphasizing is the *futility* of success just for the sake of making a name for one's self and achieving a degree of status and prestige.

I read of Dean Jones, successful film and TV actor (who portrayed Chuck Colson in the film version of the book *Born Again*). Here is a man with many prestigious credits to his name. Yet, while his beautiful canyon home was burning, he was able to sit on the front lawn and sing "Amazing Grace," much to the amazement of the firemen and arson investigators. I imagine even Dean was surprised at himself at the time. Later he was able to say, "I understood, not just at an intellectual level, but in my muscles and bones, that through praise and trusting God we can be triumphant in any circumstances...I never lost the peace of God during the whole episode. It was beautiful."

Here was a man whose house was going up in smoke, but he knew how to hang loose from it all. His happiness wasn't tied up in some bricks, timbers, and mortar — the things his success had bought for him.

There are many beautiful accounts of those who have experienced *that* kind of peace. It's a priceless treasure, and it isn't dependent upon good rave reviews in the morning paper after a performance the night before. It's not established on the shaky foundation of someone else's opinion regarding something you've said or done. Instead, God's peace is like an inner ballast which keeps you from tipping over when the storm waves of life beat against you. My husband and I have experienced it many times.

You can experience it, too. You can know what the prophet Isaiah meant when he wrote: *Thou wilt keep him in perfect peace, whose mind is stayed on thee: because he trusteth in thee* (Isaiah 26:3).

The "Roots" of the "Success Mentality"

This myth of success and prestige is encouraged through what I call the "success mentality" which pervades our culture. We have instilled into us from early childhood that some day we will grow up and be "somebody." Of course, we want our children to set high ideals and to attain to their best, and we should be glad and thankful our parents encouraged us to seek to find happiness and fulfillment in occupations and pursuits uniquely suited to our individual capabilities. This is entirely biblical. God has given each of us the ability to do certain things well (see Romans 12:6). Succeeding verses mention some of the many different vocations into which men and women are called. Previous verses urge the reader not to copy the behavior and customs of this world but to be a new and different person with a freshness about all we do and think. The promise is that then we can learn from our own experience how God's ways "will really satisfy."

But along with instilling into children the virtues of diligence and a willingness to work to achieve must be the balance of teaching them that man's final end is not just to become successful for success' sake. God has given us whatever abilities we have, and our chief end in life, as the catechism states, is to bring honor to Him and to glorify Him.

This means, among other things, that we acknowledge that what we have been endowed with in the way of creativity — any special genius or skills — has come from Him. The apostle Paul in many places emphasized that *our adequacy is from God* (see II Corinthians 3:5, for instance). Paul warns about working and doing anything out of selfishness or empty conceit (see Philippians 2:3). Paul had attained status among his contemporaries, but after his encounter with the reality of Christ, he wrote that what had preceded him thus far in his life was as *rubbish in order that* [he might] *gain Christ* (Philippians 3:8, NAS).

The supreme goal of Paul's life was to know Christ better.

This search to be "somebody" can be seen in the letters we receive in our office. Every time I join in reading them, I come away with a fresh realization that mankind is on an unending quest — the underlying theme is almost always the same. The writer has discovered that upon achieving the educational or occupational goals he established earlier in life, he has reached the desired plateau only to discover that the "certain satisfying something" he had anticipated is not there. Thus, despite success, prestige, and even material gain, he finds himself still empty and often devoid of the joy of living. Discouraged, even depressed, confused, and irritable, these individuals are writing, asking, "Why? Why am I not satisfied?"

I can assure you that if my husband and I were counting on the success we have achieved in our work to fill up the empty gaps in our lives, we would be miserable, unfulfilled individuals. The successes and prestige can be snatched away very quickly. Listen to what the Bible has to say about this: *Do not love the world, nor the things in the world. If anyone loves the world, the love of the Father is not in Him.* ***For all that is in the world, the lust of the flesh and the lust of the eyes and the boastful pride of life, is not from the Father, but is from the world. And the world is passing away, and also its lusts; but the one who does the will of God abides forever*** (I John 2:15-17, NAS, emphasis added).

Here is the answer to the "Why?"

Footnotes

1. *Webster's New World Dictionary of the American Language*, College Edition
2. Ibid.

Dealing With Depression

In the late 19th century, a man suffering from deep depression went to see a London psychiatrist. For two hours, he poured out his soul, trying desperately to explain the sense of futility that overwhelmed him. He hoped fervently that as he talked, his feelings of emptiness and desperation would somehow depart from him along with his words. He described his drained emotions and state of constant turmoil, begging the psychiatrist to say or do something that would release him from his bondage.

The psychiatrist listened knowingly. He had heard the same story many times before. In fact, he shared many of the same feelings himself but passed them off as hazards of his profession. "I am going to prescribe a rather unorthodox remedy for you," he told the man. "I want you to visit the circus."

The man looked up inquisitively.

"You need to laugh," the psychiatrist continued, "and the circus is the best place to do that."

"I don't really think that will help me — " the man began.

"Nonsense!" the doctor interrupted. "I went there myself recently. The whole experience was like a tonic to me."

"But, you see — "

"There is one particularly humorous fellow playing there: Grimaldi, the clown. Surely you've heard of him."

"Oh yes, but — "

"Why, he can make anyone laugh, and I promise it will do you much good to see him." The psychiatrist looked at his patient, whose sad eyes were beginning to form large tears.

"You don't understand," the man said.

"Of course, I do," replied the psychiatrist. "I've just spent two hours listening to you. You're suffering from depression. You could use something to make you laugh. Go see this fellow, Grimaldi."

"I am trying to tell you, sir. I *am* Grimaldi. Those antics you see are only a performance. That smile is painted on! Inside I am a miserable, empty man."

When Success Is Not Enough

The world is filled with miserable, empty, depressed people. Literally millions of Americans attempt suicide each year, playing out their dissatisfaction to its ultimate conclusion. (We talked about this somewhat in an earlier chapter.) The statistics are shocking: more than half of all suicides are teenagers, and suicide is the second leading cause of death for persons aged 13-25. Suicide is prevalent in every age group and social class but occurs more frequently in the upper-income brackets than in any other social stratum. Clearly, satisfaction cannot be guaranteed by money, prestige, fame, or even youth.

The shifting sands of popular opinion will never provide inner stability. Imagine how you would feel if you were depending on the world's acclaim to ensure your feelings of well-being and to know that you were successful if you were an actor who read in the latest *TV Guide* that you were "too old, too tall and too fat" for a certain part. Of one actress in a widely hailed television special it was written that she was "lazy," and "relying on primitive skills." That could deflate your ego incredibly fast.

If your whole idea of satisfaction and happiness in this troubled world was linked to your performance (or whatever your given role in the work-world), this type of criticism could send you into an emotional tailspin. It happens all the time. It accounts in part, researchers tell us, for the growing rate of suicides among businessmen and women. Suicide among artists and writers is quite common, and executive suicides are on the increase. Dentists lead all professions in killing themselves, followed closely by psychiatrists. And doctors are also becoming suicidal with increasing frequency. What leads successful people such as these to this kind of demise?

Dr. Herbert Klemme, director of the Division of Industrial Mental Health at the Menninger Foundation, has suggested that as a person reaches the crest of life, after 35 or so, he begins to struggle with the inevitability of his own death. He has to revise his life goals in terms of what is still possible to do. He has to be more realistic and may have to settle for a little less than he had hoped to achieve. For the person who is not reaching the goals he has set for himself, the efforts can be unsettling or even devastating.

Harvard Business Review (July, 1975), in commenting on the way so many respond to dilemmas by taking their own lives, states: "The conscientious person with high aspirations which he pursues intently is especially vulnerable to setbacks that may lead to depression and even self-destruction."

Intensely driven individuals are often very ambitious and have immense ego ideal aspirations. Oftentimes they find it difficult to relax and to express antagonism and may have an almost total lack of a sense of humor, finding it difficult to laugh at themselves or others. When life is lived under this driving pressure to succeed, they have little optimism and easily despair.

Why is depression such a pervasive force in contemporary society? Why do so many who seem to have all they could want choose to end their own lives? Why is it that with all the technological advances of the past generation, depression and dissatisfaction continue to rule the hearts and minds of the vast majority?

The answer is clear and begs to be accepted: the source of real satisfaction is a strong, abiding, personal relationship with a loving and merciful heavenly Father. No technology ever developed, no amount of money, no amount of recognition or prestige, no device or drug designed by man can ever take the place of knowing God. I am convinced that most of the depression among people in our society is directly traceable to a deep spiritual void in their lives — a void that only the Lord himself can fill. The philosopher Pascal called it "a God-shaped vacuum in every man."

How to Receive Your Heart's Desires

Psalm 37 is a rich passage of Scripture, written by David during a time when he was struggling with depression. He wrote,

> *Delight thyself also in the Lord; and he shall give thee the desires of thine heart. Commit thy way unto the Lord; trust also in him; and he shall bring it to pass* (verses 4, 5).

Contained in those short phrases is the answer to depression: *Delight thyself . . . in the Lord.* They also reveal a wonderful promise that deals with the challenge of dissatisfaction: *He shall give thee the desires of thine heart.*

What does it mean to delight yourself in the Lord? Simply to turn your focus away from yourself, or, in the words of the apostle Paul, to *Set your affection on things above, not on things on the earth* (Colossians 3:2). It means to make your relationship with God the central issue in your life — to desire to know Him, fellowship with Him, and live for His glory more than anything else.

Frances Kelley, co-anchor for a daily morning news program on a Memphis television station, was kind enough to allow me to interview her on our telecast. She told a touching personal story about her rise from poverty to become a successful but dissatisfied entertainment personality.

As a young black girl growing up in the South, Frances faced many hardships. Still, she was determined to break out of poverty and find success. When she was old enough, she left home and became a nightclub singer. She married and moved to New York and then Detroit, where she lived in a large house with all the benefits of material success. She had cars, clothes, servants — everything but real satisfaction.

Frances told me, "One day I remembered a little black girl standing in her grandparents' coal house with the sunshine streaming through the slats, looking up, knowing there was a God on the other end somewhere up there. Now, as an adult, seemingly lacking nothing, I felt just like that little girl again in some respects, and the tears ran down my cheeks. Here I was, standing in my beautiful, big house, looking up, knowing there was a God somewhere but not knowing how to reach Him. I felt there was nothing to live for. On the outside, to anyone looking at me and our life-style, it would appear I had it made. I'd tasted success. My husband was a well-to-do businessman. But all I felt was emptiness. I was so dissatisfied with myself.

"I was trying to drink myself into oblivion. I even tried suicide and failed in the attempt. I was mad at God because I thought He was unkind not to let me die.

"About that time a young man in the neighborhood came by to visit and told me about a church he was starting nearby. Eventually, I found my way to that little church. Someone opened the Bible to me at Jeremiah 32:27, where I read, *Behold, I am the Lord, the God of all flesh: is there any thing too hard for me?*

"I realized there wasn't anything too hard for God. I presented my case, the Holy Spirit took it to the 'court of God,' and we won! Glory! Hallelujah! Now I am a Christian when I go to bed at night; I am a Christian when I wake up in the morning. Now what I am is tied up in Christ. Now I am a satisfied woman."

What success, prestige, and money were not able to give Frances Kelley, she discovered in a relationship with the living God. He gave her the real desire of her heart — peace and the assurance of eternal life.

I believe there is a dual meaning to the promise that God will give us our hearts' desires. First, it means that He will fulfill our deepest longings — not the desires we have for things, but our desire for spiritual wholeness. Every human being, whether he is aware of it or not, has deep spiritual needs, and only God can satisfy them. He does that for those who delight themselves in Him.

The promise also means that God will place new desires and aspirations in our hearts. When He makes us spiritually whole, He gives us new priorities, new values — new desires. He gives us holy desires, desires for spiritual blessings, desires that only He can fulfill. And He delights in fulfilling them.

Frances Kelley is only one of millions who have found the answer to dissatisfaction and depression. In our years of evangelistic ministry, we have been privileged to point thousands to the way of salvation. And we are constantly thrilled and amazed to see how the Lord transforms lives.

Sometimes, an experience is so dramatic and poignant that I am reminded anew of how amazing God's love for us really is, and how wonderfully timely His grace is to those who need it most. Such an incident occurred one night several years ago in Grand Rapids, Michigan. We were conducting a citywide crusade there, and I was on the platform prior to the service, getting the music ready. Suddenly, I noticed one of our counselors motioning that he would like to speak to me. He seemed to have something urgent to say, so I started a tape of background music and turned my attention to him.

"My wife and I were on our way to the service, when we saw a young woman jump from the bridge near the auditorium," he told me breathlessly. "We rushed to the edge of the river and saw that she was struggling to get out of the water."

My heart was pounding as I listened. He continued, "She made her way up to the shore, and my wife held her in her arms while I ran and phoned for an ambulance. By the time I had returned, my wife had told her about God's love for her and Jesus' death on the cross for people just like her." The man told us that there, beside what could have been her watery grave, she found everlasting life by trusting Christ.

God's timing was perfect. Not only did that couple

arrive at the bridge just in time to save the woman's life, but according to God's perfect plan, they were able to give her something to live for as well. The salvation she received that night was not only salvation from a watery grave, but also salvation from an eternity without God.

Depression and dissatisfaction are not necessarily limited to those who do not know the Lord or who are walking out of His will. Interestingly, the great prophet Elijah also encountered this problem. Even more amazing is the fact that Elijah's depression hit him just after a great spiritual victory. In I Kings 18, we see Elijah winning a great contest against the prophets of Baal. God was vindicated, and the false prophets were destroyed. Yet in chapter 19, just days after this victory, we find Elijah pleading with God to take his life.

Part of Elijah's problem, I'm sure, was that he was physically and emotionally exhausted. Therefore, the first thing God did was allow him to eat, sleep, and regain his strength (verses 4-9). Then, God spoke to him, listened to his complaints, encouraged him, and sent him right back to work! We can learn much from Elijah's battle with depression.

Physical Causes for Depression

First, depression may have a physical cause. Beware — Satan loves to take advantage of us when we become physically exhausted. Therefore, we should take time daily to exercise, rest, and guard our health by eating properly. We have had Judy McFarland on our program twice — Judy and her mother Gladys

Lindberg co-authored the book *Take Charge of Your Health*. She helped us understand the relationship between good physical health and good mental and emotional health. It's terribly important. God has equipped our bodies with a wonderful healing system capable of handling almost any condition — provided it is given the nutritional support it needs. Judy says one essential fact must be understood if people are to maintain physical and emotional health: the state of their nutrition directly influences their biochemistry and their immunological system. There are many misunderstood health problems that go misdiagnosed because a lot of medical people still refuse to recognize the correlation between nutrition and health.

I'm glad that Jack and I recognized this long ago. Both of us enjoy bicycle riding and exercise regularly. And we know that the stress and wear and tear on our bodies caused by the kind of lives most of us lead today necessitates that we eat properly. Also, there are so many contaminants in the environment and in the foods we all consume that we urge people to pay attention to well-informed people like Judy and her mother Gladys Lindberg (highly respected nutritionists living on the West Coast). When we take care of our bodies (mental and physical health), we are cooperating with the Creator. There is much said in the Bible on this important subject.

Spiritual Causes of Depression

Second, you may be attempting to wage the battle of life totally in the flesh, leaving God, His providence, and His power out of the picture. Christians, especially, who should know better, must guard against running counter to or ahead of the Lord. I have long cherished and drawn comfort from the blessed promise contained in Proverbs 3:5,6: *Trust in the Lord with all thine heart; and lean not unto thine own understanding. In all thy ways acknowledge him, and he shall direct thy paths.*

Yes, we must allow Him to do the leading and, as we follow, refusing to be discouraged by fear or failure, we will find we can handle the stressful situations that come into our lives that might otherwise leave us depressed and overwhelmed.

Christians, of all people, should be the most satisfied in all the world. This isn't always the case, however, and, sadly, is a poor commentary on our relationship to the very One who provides help and hope. I think it has a lot to do with the fact that we don't want to admit that these "black nights of the soul" do come to us, and when they do, we fail to turn to the Lord, committing our way to Him, trusting Him, and acknowledging that we need His help and direction.

Go to the Top for Help

Third, and finally, once you have recognized that you have a problem, don't give up and simply drown in your depression. Realize that you need help, consider the causes, and then begin looking for answers.

If the problem is physical, get medical help immediately!

If it is spiritual, take it to the Lord. Remember His

compassionate invitation in Matthew 11:28, given to everyone: *Come unto me, all ye that labour and are heavy laden, and I will give you rest.* If personal counseling is required, go to your pastor. Or if the problem seems to be unusually deep-seated, see a Christian psychologist.

Above all, don't make the mistake of taking comfort in self-pity — of thinking that you are alone. Elijah did. He said, *I, even I only, am left* (I Kings 19:10). But he was not really alone. God was on his side. Furthermore, God had seven thousand faithful people in Israel who had not bowed the knee to Baal — and all were looking to Elijah for leadership! What an encouragement to overcome disillusionment and depression.

Somebody needs your help and leadership, too. You cannot afford to dwell in the pits of self-pity and depression. You must look beyond yourself, past your problems, to God, who is greater than them all. His love for you is deep and unending, and if you trust Him — if you delight yourself in Him — He will give you the desires of your heart. That is His unfaltering promise.

Section III

Finding True Satisfaction

Grace to the Humble

There seems to be a paradox in the fact that there are many people who seemingly enjoy outward success in terms of money, recognition, and prestige, despite the fact that they are not truly humble. However, the blessing of God is not measured by immediate or outward accomplishments. Let us examine this more carefully.

The life of pioneer missionary David Livingstone is beautiful proof of this. When Livingstone was a young man, he informed his brother that he planned to become a missionary. His brother scoffed, saying that he preferred to remain in England, seeking fame and fortune. He wanted recognition from his peers, and that was not possible, he said, for a missionary in Africa.

David went to Africa, where he labored untiringly among the people as a doctor and preacher. The Lord gave him the desires of his heart, and many people came to know Jesus Christ under his ministry. His brother, who stayed in England, did indeed find fame and recognition and accumulated a great amount of wealth as well.

When David Livingstone died, his heart was buried in Africa and his body shipped home to England for burial in Westminster Cathedral. Later, his brother was buried next to him. We visited this great edifice a few years ago, and my heart was deeply touched as I read the inscriptions on the brothers' graves. On the site where David Livingstone was buried is this poem:

DAVID LIVINGSTONE

He needs no epitaph to guard a name
Which men shall prize while worthy work is known;
He lived and died for good — be that his fame:
Let marble crumble; this is Living — stone.

The inscription above his brother's grave simply states: "Charles, the brother of David Livingstone." This illustration, more than any I know, reflects the truth of I Peter 5:6: *Humble yourselves therefore under the mighty hand of God, that he may exalt you in due time.*

The First Shall Be Last

No attitude or character quality was more emphasized and exemplified by the Lord Jesus than was humility. He told His disciples, *...whosoever will be great among you, let him be your minister; And whosoever will be chief among you, let him be your servant* (Matthew 20:26-27).

Shortly after He gave that lesson, He met with His disciples in an upper room to eat what we have come to call the Last Supper. In those final hours before He was taken away to be tortured and killed, Jesus, knowing what He would have to bear, took time to teach His disciples one more lesson about the importance of humility.

As they entered the room where they would eat that final meal together, they found that everything had been prepared for them, with one exception — a servant to wash their feet. In those days of dirt roads and sandals, washing feet regularly was an essential custom. Since it was not a pleasant chore, it was normally the duty of the lowest slave when an individual entered a house.

After everything Jesus had taught His disciples about humility, it would seem that one of them should have volunteered to accept the responsibility — or at least found a slave willing to do it. However, none did. Perhaps they were involved in one of their arguments about which of them was the greatest.

Consequently, Jesus rolled up His sleeves, took the basin of water and a towel, stooped down, and began to wash the disciples' feet. They were so shocked at His actions that they became speechless. Jesus told them: *Ye call me Master and Lord: and ye say well; for so I am. If I then, your Lord and Master, have washed your feet; ye also ought to wash one another's feet. For I have given you an example, that ye should do as I have done to you* (John 13:13-15).

There is a great and important lesson here for all of us. If Jesus could leave heaven and come to earth to die and on the night before His crucifixion assume a position of the lowliest of slaves, without reservation, we ought to follow His example of humility.

False Humility

Have you ever met someone who seemed to exhibit a kind of false humility which does not in any way glorify the Lord? It is lowliness put on to impress others. It is not a genuine humility but rather a shallow, external facade that actually seeks to put others down. This false humility takes various forms. For example, by refusing to graciously accept a compliment (how embarrassing to the one who is giving it) and discrediting ones own accomplishments, they are actually seeking to draw more praise to themselves. This is pride in disguise — not a meekness of spirit.

Such hypocritical humility is like the sin of the Pharisees. They put on sackcloth and ashes when they fasted so that everyone could see how "spiritual" they were. They would stand on the street corners to pray, just to make certain that no one missed their display of holiness. What they really wanted was the praise of men, and Jesus said that was all the reward they would get for their human efforts.

Humility that calls attention to itself is not humility at all — it is pride. And what makes pride so insidious is that we are most vulnerable to it just when we think we have conquered it. The minute we begin thinking how humble we are, we had better think again. No one who considers himself a paragon of humility knows the first thing about the virtue.

On the other side of the coin, however, neither is a poor self-image the same thing as humility. I have known people who did not like themselves very much, but they were so self-centered that they made it difficult for anyone else to like them. The truly humble person can accept himself. He feels good about himself because he is not consumed by the desire to prove himself to others — to convince others that he is something he is not.

The Essence of True Humility

What constitutes true humility? Jesus himself answered this question when He washed the feet of His disciples at the Last Supper. Genuine humility is, you see, *a willingness to serve others*.

Nothing is more lonely than a "self-service only" individual. (We seem to keep coming back to that truth, don't we?) In fact, the most dissatisfied persons I know are those who are selfish. Because they are so wrapped up in themselves — their own needs, their own desires, their own preferences, their own problems — they cannot reach out to others for the very fellowship that would dispel their loneliness.

Of all the disciples, Andrew best pictures the meaning of true humility. Andrew had a servant's heart. He does not seem to have been involved as James and John were in the constant disputes about who was the greatest. Instead, whenever we see

Andrew in Scripture, he is bringing someone else to the Master.

Andrew began his ministry of soulwinning and discipleship by seeking Peter, his brother. In fact, perhaps the greatest thing that Andrew ever did was bring Peter to Jesus. Peter became the leader of the disciples, and after Jesus ascended into heaven, it was Peter who preached the great sermon at Pentecost where so many were converted to faith in Christ.

If you had a brother like Peter, would you have brought him to Jesus? Surely Andrew knew that Peter, with his domineering personality, would inherit the position of leadership among the disciples. He must have realized that he would eventually take a back seat to his brother. Yet Andrew was not concerned with those things. He saw only his brother's need and knew that Jesus could fill it. In a sense, Andrew did fade into the shadows as Peter came into prominence. But he also continued to bring others to Jesus. One of those he brought was a little boy with a sack lunch — and the Lord used that lunch to feed a multitude. Take heart — your seemingly small talent can be used and magnified for His glory, because God both desires and rewards humble service.

God Gives Grace to the Humble

What does humility have to do with satisfaction? Humility is a channel through which the Lord can bless us. Pride, on the other hand, isolates us from God. I Peter 5:5 urges, . . . *be clothed with humility: for God resisteth the proud, and giveth grace to the humble.*

God's grace is manifested in a special way to those who are humble. If a person seeks to serve others, he receives multiplied blessings from the Lord. If he seeks only to serve self, however, he closes the door to the possibility of such blessings.

Too many who claim to be working for the Lord see the ministry only as a platform on which to display their own talents and abilities. My husband and I believe that our service constitutes a high and holy privilege, and our prayer has always been that God be glorified in all that we say and do — not only in public, but in our private lives as well.

As a result of this belief, we have always felt strongly that we should not push open doors to try to expand our ministry. Everywhere we have gone and in every situation in which we have ministered, we have endeavored to wait until God himself opened the portals of increased opportunity. In fact, sometimes we have been so cautious that He has had to push us through them! Still, the peace of mind and soul we have experienced in knowing that God has brought each new phase of our outreach to pass far outweighs any sense of human accomplishment. It also confirms in our hearts the fact that *Except the Lord build the house, they labor in vain that build it* (Psalm 127:1).

Through our years of ministry together, I have also appreciated and learned from Jack's meek and tender spirit. When we conducted our local church and citywide crusades, we were inevitably the last ones to leave the auditorium following a service. My husband always had time to answer one more question or sign an additional Bible, no matter how late the hour. As I stood by him, often ministering with him, my heart smiled within me to know that this one who had the power to deliver such authoritative and convicting messages from God's Word also had the ability to understand the deepest burdens and personally minister to the hearts he touched. Today, our office doors are open to students, pastors, and young evangelists who seek to share the wisdom, counsel, and direction the Lord has given us in conducting our international ministry.

One thing we attempt to impress on the minds of those we meet — especially persons just entering the ministry — is the fact that the word *ministry* itself means *service*. A minister is a servant, and no one is truly ministering if he does not have a servant's heart. No one who is unwilling to get his hands dirty washing the feet of another is worthy to be called a servant of God.

I shall never forget our very first visit to Tennessee Temple Schools in Chattanooga. Jack and I were tremendously excited (and a bit nervous) about ministering in a college environment, not to mention being in the presence of such a respected man as Dr. Lee Roberson, the president. I had never met him and was anxious to make his acquaintance.

We arrived in the city several hours ahead of time and drove to the auditorium in order to unload and set up our equipment. We were met by several students and staff members, including a distinguished-looking, gray-haired gentleman who helped us carry the heavy pieces to the platform.

Much time was spent placing everything into position, making the proper electrical connections, and testing for operation and sound level. At last our task was completed. I turned to the gray-haired gentleman and thanked him for his assistance. "And when shall we be able to meet Dr. Roberson?" I asked.

The man smiled softly and gently took hold of my hand. "I am Dr. Roberson," he replied.

That evening, as Dr. Lee Roberson stepped to the podium to welcome the students and guests and introduce us to them, he appeared ever so much taller, broad-shouldered, and distinguished. Silently, I bowed my head and prayed a prayer of rejoicing, thanking God for allowing me the privilege of meeting a true servant of the Lord Jesus Christ.

There is a great deal of true satisfaction in service for others. The servant of God is actually a kind of funnel through which God pours out His love to a needy world. The person who is involved in humble service is vibrant and alive. He can sense the love of God flowing through him, and he is constantly getting a firsthand experience of the way God works.

In addition, the truly humble person has all his relationships in proper perspective. He does not think more highly of himself than he ought to think (see Romans 12:3). He does not look down on others, use them for his own benefit, or ignore their needs. Most important, he is in right relationship to God.

God Hates Pride

Many of us are familiar with the children's story about the frog who wanted to fly. As he sat on his lily pad watching for insects day after day, he often spied the birds of the forest gracefully winging their way through the air. Their freedom and ability to travel quickly from one place to another began to disturb him, and he soon became completely dissatisfied with his lot in life. He wanted to fly.

One day the frog went to his friend, the Robin. "Mr. Robin, will you teach me to fly?" he asked.

"I'm sorry, but that's impossible," said the Robin. "You're a frog. Frogs were not created to fly. Frogs were made to hop."

Next, the frog approached the Cardinal. "Mr. Cardinal, please teach me to fly," he pleaded. To his dismay, the reply was the same.

Then the frog conceived a brilliant idea. He hopped to the Robin and to the Cardinal. "Robin, Cardinal!" he shouted enthusiastically. "I have the answer! If you two will pick up a stick and hold it tightly in your beaks, I will grab the stick with my mouth and travel with you as you fly."

Although somewhat skeptical, the frog's feathered friends agreed to give his idea a try. They found a sturdy stick, grasped it tightly in their beaks, and the frog did likewise. Then off they flew — up, up, higher and higher, swiftly skirting the trees of the forest, out across the meadow and back once more.

The frog was jubilant. He was flying!

One by one, the animals appeared at the forest's edge, gazing in disbelief at the sight before them. As the triumphant trio made another sweep past the crowd of spectators, the deer exclaimed: "How clever! Who ever conceived such a perfectly ingenius idea?"

The frog, swelling with pride, shouted, "I did! It was all *my* idea!"

As he spoke, he lost his grip on the stick and

hurtled through the air to the ground. Splat! Alas, the frog's dream and delight proved to be his demise. His life was snuffed out in a moment of time. The sin of pride had claimed another victim — just as it will claim you and me if we do not face it openly and honestly and allow it to remain unchecked in our lives.

Remember, God says, *Pride goeth before destruction, and an haughty spirit before a fall* (Proverbs 16:18).

Why is pride so deadly? For one thing, pride was the sin that led to Satan's fall. Caught up with his own beauty and wisdom, willfully forgetting the fact that it was God who made him that way, Lucifer began to see himself as something to be worshipped above God. When he said: *I will be like the most High* (Isaiah 14:14), he lost everything that was his.

Later, Satan succeeded in getting Eve to sin with the same promise with which he had deceived himself: *. . . ye shall be as gods* (Genesis 3:5). And when Adam and Eve sinned, they too lost everything God had given to them. Most devastating of all, they were sent forth from His presence. Ever since that day, the human race has been plagued by the sin of pride and the consequent loss of blessing that comes with it. Like the frog, humanity desperately seeks satisfaction but at the same time stubbornly refuses to renounce the pride that makes dissatisfaction inevitable.

Some would have us believe that pride is a virtue. In recent years, a number of best-selling books have appeared, telling us how to assert ourselves, how to get what we want, how to increase our self-esteem, and how to intimidate others. Humility is viewed by many as a weakness. The "me-first" syndrome has spread throughout society like a plague.

In such an atmosphere, it is little wonder that so many are dissatisfied, for it is in giving, not receiving that we are blessed. It is in serving, not being served, that life finds it depth. And it is in humility, not pride, that we open ourselves to receive the grace of God.

God hates this sin of pride (see Proverbs 8:13). Pride is a denial of God's right to glory. It is a challenge to His sovereignty. It is a deification of self over God, and it leads to contempt for others for whom Christ died. It is as morally perverse and debasing as any sin known to man, for it can lead to many other kinds of sin.

How damaging and hurtful pride is! It increases the desire for satisfaction and at the same time pushes the possibility of personal fulfillment further and further away. May God give us the grace to be truly humble.

Sowing and Reaping

What are some of the major hindrances to satisfaction? What are the things that cause so many people to be dissatisfied? The answers I am going to suggest may surprise you, for I do not believe the deepest kinds of dissatisfaction have external causes. Most of us have known people who have faced diversified and devastating trials without losing their sense of satisfaction.

The real source of dissatisfaction, I believe, is *within* an individual. Those who struggle with bitterness, jealousy, or guilt (sins of the spirit), for example, are more prone to dissatisfaction than those who have resolved their internal struggles. One verse in the Bible gives the reason for this phenomenon: *. . . whatsoever a man soweth, that shall he also reap* (Galatians 6:7).

The principle of sowing and reaping is one that every gardener understands. If you plant watermelon seeds, you cannot expect to harvest corn. Roses will not grow from a tulip bulb, etc.

The same principle is true in every area of life. If a person smokes and drinks to excess, he will reap the bitter fruit of it in physical and family problems. If a person uses mind-dulling drugs, he may permanently damage his brain. A person who engages in promiscuity leaves himself open to venereal disease — including herpes and AIDS — emotional disorders, and many other permanent ailments. The one who sows wickedness will always reap destructive consequences.

On the other hand, if one sows the seeds of righteousness, he reaps beautiful and fulfilling benefits. A person who sows kindness reaps the same. One who speaks graciously of others is graciously spoken of in return. The more we give, the more we receive. Many illustrations of the universal principle of sowing and reaping could be cited.

Sowing Seeds of Kindness

I have always marveled that so many people seem not to understand this elementary principle of life. When I was very young, my father applied this truth to my life in such a way that it never left me. He heard me say something unkind to someone and took me aside, telling me of an incident during his childhood in Missouri. He had his own horse and was trying to get it to do something it was determined not to do. Consequently, he took a stick and began to whip it. However, the harder he struck the horse, the more resolute the animal became.

His mother had been inside watching and soon came out with a handful of sugar cubes. "Rex," she said, "you will find that this will work better than the switch." And it did! From that day on, he treated his horse with love and affection, and he never again had trouble getting it to do what he wanted.

"People are like horses," my father told me. "They respond better to affection than to brutality. People are drawn to love. They are starved for it."

That day I resolved never again to treat anyone with unkindness — and I have tried never to forget that lesson!

What joy there is in being kind to others! At the department store, in the supermarket, in the post office — even in traffic, the law of sowing and reaping is in effect. How you respond to people determines how they will respond to you. Remember, you are making relationships that can bring either satisfaction or dissatisfaction, and the difference is determined by the kind of attitude you sow.

Jesus said: *As ye would that men should do to you, do ye also to them likewise* (Luke 6:31). In its common form, we know this as the Golden Rule: "Do unto others as you would have them do unto you." The modern version, however, has become, "Do unto others *before* they do unto you," and this mentality is responsible for much of the dissatisfaction of contemporary man.

Satisfaction Through Serving Others

What are some other seeds that, if planted in the heart, bring forth the fruit of dissatisfaction? In the last chapter we talked about pride. Closely related to pride is the attitude of *selfishness*. Much of the world's dissatisfaction, I am convinced, is directly traceable to the "me first" syndrome that has swept society in the past few decades.

Books with titles like *Looking Out for Number One*, and *Winning Through Intimidation* rise instantly to the top of the best-seller list. Several years ago the nation was outraged at the story of a young girl in New York who was raped, brutalized, and murdered while a crowd watched. No one lifted a finger to help her — no one even called the police! Today, such stories are common news items. Nobody wants to get involved. Fewer and fewer people care enough about their neighbors to take risks. The needs of others are becoming secondary to our own, and this apathetic mentality is strangling our society.

Jesus taught that it is more blessed to give than to receive. Do you really want to be happy? Give. Help meet the needs of others. Truly there is more satisfaction in showing love to someone than there is in receiving another person's love. This is the secret of building solid human relationships and a sense of accomplishment and self-worth.

Concern for others is one of the qualities that helped build our nation and has made the United States great. Commenting on this American distinctive, Barbara Bush, wife of Vice President George Bush, told me in a 1982 interview: "Our willingness to share is what makes us different from other countries. When George was at the United Nations, I used to work two mornings a week at Memorial Sloan-Kettering Cancer Center. All the ambassadors' wives would say to me, 'Do you work for nothing?' I said, 'Yes, I love it.' They said, 'We don't understand that. That's what makes your country different, isn't it? To care about other people.'" Barbara Bush is one of those special people who exudes a genuine concern for others. She practices Galatians 6:2: *Bear ye one another's burdens, and so fulfil the law of Christ.*

I believe one of the first places this principle should be applied is in the home. This is one important reason Jack and I have had such a rewarding and wonderful relationship all these years. He seems to actually enjoy doing things for me, always caring about my needs and my concerns. And I delight in returning his attentiveness with my love, devotion, and gratitude. We relish and appreciate each other's presence and (heaven forbid) never take it for granted. Simply stated, we enjoy each other.

A very ordinary example is Jack's quickness to open doors for me. That may seem like a small, mundane thing, just a basic part of good manners. Still, it is becoming more and more unusual to see a man open a door for his wife. Jack doesn't do it because I *demand* it but because it is one of the little ways he shows me his love. He enjoys treating me like someone special. If I began to take it for granted, or worse yet, to insist on it, the gesture would cease to be meaningful. If I began to say, "Now, Jack, we're coming to a door. You get up there and open it for me," I'm sure he would soon begin to grow weary of obeying me, and I could no longer rejoice in his graciousness.

A person who thinks he *deserves* to be served

cannot appreciate what others do for him. When we have a servant's heart, however, we are able to truly enjoy both serving and being served. When we serve someone with the right heart attitude, we are doing what we love, and when someone serves us, it is an unexpected delight.

The Real Problem — Sin

The greatest culprit of all in stealing satisfaction away from men and women is sin. This may seem like an old-fashioned concept in our modern age, but after years of changing standards and in spite of society's attempts to explain away most sins, people must still deal with the enormous guilt that always comes when we violate God's standards.

It doesn't matter, for example, that our courts have said that abortion upon demand is now legal. Literally millions of women who have had abortions, without consideration of the life they have obliterated, suffer from feelings of guilt every time they look at a baby. Oh, that they would have considered an alternative.

It doesn't matter that society has sanctioned divorce for *any cause*. People who have used divorce as an easy way out are finding that it is not really pleasant to deal with their lingering misgivings. It doesn't matter that chastity before marriage and marital fidelity no longer seem important in our culture. Young people who sin this way invariably face the pangs of regret that come with having transgressed God's laws.

Al Palmquist is a former policeman who helps

young girls who have become prostitutes break away from their lives of sin. His book, *The Minnesota Connection*, tells how he helped break one of the nation's largest prostitution rings. Al has been on our television program a number of times. He says that to try to get away from the guilt that goes with their life-style, prostitutes must turn either to drugs or alcohol or some other form of escapism. Many of them sit and watch television all day to get their minds off their guilt.

Prostitutes are not the only ones who practice this kind of escapism. Others, perhaps with more socially acceptable sins, also find themselves unable to deal with the problem of guilt. As a result they, too, turn to drugs, television, or some other form of escape.

But escapism cannot satisfy. Instead, it only changes one form of misery into another. Those who have sowed the seeds of sin soon discover that they must indeed reap the ultimate harvest. Cruelly, sin, which always promises satisfaction, gives only temporary pleasure and then inevitably destroys the possibility of real satisfaction.

A New Start

What those suffering from the effects of sin really need is a new start. God has not left us hopeless. He promises that a new beginning is possible, and He has provided a way to break the endless cycle of sowing and reaping, sin and misery.

The third chapter of John's gospel records the interesting yet tragic story of a frustrated religious leader in Jesus' day. His name was Nicodemus. As a member of Israel's strictest religious sect (the Pharisees), Nicodemus observed every jot and tittle of the law and helped set the standards of religious worship and service. Yet his own heart was deeply troubled.

Nicodemus had observed the Lord, taking careful note of His person, teaching, and works. He knew that Christ was no ordinary man and longed for a deeper understanding of His divine teaching. More importantly, he recognized that Jesus could provide the answer to the void that filled his own soul — how to inherit eternal life. Because of his pride and position, he came to the Saviour secretly, under the cover of darkness (verse 2).

Jesus told Nicodemus that such a new beginning was not only possible but absolutely essential for everyone who seeks true satisfaction. He said: *Except a man be born again, he cannot see the kingdom of God* (verse 3). Elaborating on this new birth, available only through Christ, II Corinthians 5:17 declares: *Therefore if any man be in Christ, he is a new creature: old things are passed away; behold,* ***all things are become new*** (emphasis added).

Yes, God makes it possible for us not only to begin anew, but also to reap the fruit of the righteousness Jesus Christ has sown. Because He died for our sins — reaping the penalty for that which we have sown — we can receive eternal life, as well as peace and satisfaction in our earthly lives.

This is God's provision for satisfaction, and it works! Why? Because it deals with the real cause of dissatisfaction — the problems within the human heart. Through the years that we have been in the

Lord's service, we have had the privilege of seeing scores of people come to Christ to get a new start in life. All of them will testify that nothing is more satisfying than knowing the Lord and yielding completely to Him.

One woman in particular comes to my mind at this time. I saw her sitting on the front row during a service one night. She had four beautiful children with her, and she had been in the same place every evening of the crusade. She watched Jack intently while he preached, and I remember thinking that she seemed like a drowning woman waiting for a life raft to come her way. I was not surprised when she stepped forward during the invitation to receive Christ as her Saviour.

Several weeks later we received a letter telling us of this woman's newfound joy in the Lord and her desire to tell others of the way of salvation and true satisfaction. At the time of our crusade, she was unemployed, and the courts had stripped her of legal custody of her children. (In fact, she stated that the family had walked three miles to attend the services each night.)

After she received Christ, everything just seemed to fall into place in her life. First, she found a lasting joy she never knew possible. Then, she witnessed a miracle. Standing before the judge, she told him that she had been born again and that regardless of whether she received custody of her children, she was going to live for the Lord. She said, however, she would praise the Lord throughout all eternity if she had the opportunity to rear them for Him.

"I really think you mean it," the judge said, and he

gave her that opportunity.

The woman found a good church to attend, and her life and the lives of her children began to touch others with the marvelous truth that God can indeed give a new start.

The situation does not always change that quickly for everyone. (I realize that.) However, when Jesus comes into a life, He removes the guilt, the bitterness, the selfishness, and all the other heart problems that stand in the way of true satisfaction. In their place as one yields, He puts the fruit of the Spirit— love, joy, peace, patience, gentleness, goodness, faith, meekness, and self-control. Then as we follow Him by faith, we begin to experience a deep satisfaction that nothing can ever remove. It should be admitted and recognized that this doesn't always happen immediately. Sometimes it takes time for old habits to disappear, and so you should not despair. Give God time to work in your life, and give yourself time. I like what the apostle Peter had to say about this. He suggested that like a newborn baby, the new person in Christ should crave spiritual milk so that by it he might become mature in the faith (see I Peter 2:2). Remember, He will never fail to complete the work He has begun (see I Corinthians 1:8).

How Can My Marriage Be Better?

Someone told me recently that he thought it would be difficult to be friendly toward, and become genuinely interested in, each of the guests I interview on our weekly television program! I replied that it is not an act with me — I thoroughly enjoy meeting these people and listening to their fascinating accounts. I have had the privilege of interviewing many well-known personalities — people who have been used to touching lives through politics, the sciences, the arts, and literature.

One of the most memorable authors I have been privileged to interview on the telecast is Florence Littauer. She gave a fascinating account of her wedding. Like most young ladies, Florence had long dreamed of the day she would be married. She was employed as a high school drama teacher when she became engaged to a wonderful young man, so she decided to let her pupils participate in planning and arranging some of the details of her wedding. "Everybody worked," she told me. "We had the auto shop boys find a white Cadillac; the wood shop boys made scepters for the bridesmaids; and, of course, I was the queen. My students wrote to *Life Magazine* suggesting they come and cover their teacher's wedding."

Both Florence and her students were surprised when reporters and photographers from *Life* actually appeared! For weeks they followed Florence around, taking notes and pictures. The wedding was a dream come true, and being chosen by *Life Magazine* as bride of the year only made it better.

But, Florence told me, her marriage that began with so much fanfare soon ran into serious trouble. Only with the Lord's help, much prayer, and a great deal of growth in the life of her husband and herself was the couple able to overcome the weaknesses in their crumbling marriage and rebuild it stronger than ever. Now Florence has written a book, appropriately titled, *After Every Wedding Comes a Marriage.* Based on her experiences, as well as my own, I am focusing this chapter on the special ingredients that are vital to a successful and happy marriage.

Unconditional Love

In counseling those with marital problems, I've noticed that dissatisfaction often seems to center in the family life. For example, a husband who undergoes unusual stress at work frequently shows the effects of that stress in his relationship with his wife. Likewise, a wife who is dissatisfied may focus her feelings of depression and resentment on her husband. Consequently, one of the first casualties of dissatisfaction is often the *marriage*.

I believe the quality of one's love is a barometer of the state of the marriage. When the marital "love level" (I especially like this term) declines, coldness in the relationship sets in. Wives, your husbands are the *last* ones who should bear the brunt of your dissatisfaction. Husbands, the same is true of your wives. Why is it, then, that the ones we should love most are often the first to feel the heat of our negative feelings? The final person with whom we should be short of temper is our spouse, and yet so often the reverse is true. In fact, a popular song from many decades ago was titled, "You Always Hurt the One You Love," as if that makes everything all right.

Genuine love demands an unconditional commitment and requires a daily, conscious effort in order to grow stronger. Because this is especially true in the marriage relationship, those looking for an easy way out will not experience success in matrimony. I have advised many women that they must be willing to do whatever is necessary to make their marriage rewarding. "*Work* at it," I tell them. Some of the best advice I ever received came early in my own marriage: "Love your husband. It will put iron in his spine." I've made that my philosophy, and it has worked. Thus, I tell those who seek my help, "Love your mate when it's easy, and love him when it's not. Love him unconditionally."

Unfeigned love, you see, begets more love because we are all responders. So as the partners commit themselves to showing love toward each other, the relationship blossoms and grows in strength and beauty.

Too many people view love as something that must be earned or deserved. Yet, love that is not unconditional is not really love at all. The essence of God's divine nature is love — unconditional love. He loved us *in spite* of our shortcomings. In fact, He loved us so much He sent His Son to *die* for us.

Love is More Than a Feeling

Without a doubt the most misunderstood word in all the world is *love*. This is probably due to the misconception created by the lyrics of much of our contemporary music as well as the way love, divorce, and sex is exploited through some television programs and movies. Love, you see, is more than a feeling of selfish emotions, but as I have already suggested, it is the ability to place one's selfish interest and feelings aside to give to another person.

In the English language there is but one word — love — to cover every emotion from lust to sacrificial devotion. With this in mind, few are aware that there are different meanings of the word *love* in the Bible as discovered in the original Hebrew and Greek texts. The first Greek word is *eros*. It is the root word for our English word *erotic*. This is the type of love which most of us have experienced at one time or another, probably in our early teens.

Remember when you felt it the first time? You thought you were walking on air. Later, you realized it was what your parents called "puppy love" or infatuation. I am sorry to say that this can sometimes lead to strong sexual stimulation and eroticism which produces premarital sex, even premarital pregnancies, and progress to marriage without the maturity and growth of true love.

The second kind of love comes from the Greek word *philia. Philia* is friendship, companionship leading to a desire to cooperate and share time and interests with others. In marriage it depicts a husband and wife or parents and children working together. They enjoy each others company. The difference then between *eros* and *philia* love is that *eros* is a face-to-face encounter while *philia* is a shoulder-to-shoulder relationship. These two words however do not tell the entire story of love in its fullest beauty.

There is a final word in the Greek that enables us to understand the *deepest meaning of love.* It is *agape love. Eros* love produces romance between two people and *philia* love makes two people enjoy one another as friends. But the greatest of these — *agape* love — makes one give his all, even his life for another. It produces total commitment and selflessness within hearts and lives. This is God's *agape* love for us.

Don't be fooled by emotions or friendly feelings, calling them love, but be absolutely sure of the quality and depth of your love for the one you would marry. The perfect marriage incorporates all three of these aspects of love into one beautiful commitment.

Frequently I hear men and women claim that love has gone out of their marriage. To me, this is always a clue to the fact that they really do not understand the nature of love. What they mean, perhaps, is that they have lost the warm, emotional feeling they once had toward their spouse. Remember, love is not just a warm, emotional feeling but an unconditional commitment to the good of another.

If real love is present in a marriage, it can never be lost. The feelings that accompany it may be sorely tested — even assaulted, imposed upon — but I Corinthians 13-type love is able to bear all things. Nothing can destroy it. Thus it will remain regardless of one's emotions and irrespective of circumstances.

Don't Try to Change Your Spouse

Too many people marry their spouses thinking that they can change the other person into someone more to their likes and dislikes. Florence Littauer told me that if this were possible, she and her husband, Fred, would have done it. "I set out to make Fred fun like me," she said, "and Fred was determined to get me organized like him." Her advice to those trying to change their partners? "*It won't work.*" Disillusionment and discouragement are bound to result, and ultimately the marriage will flounder and may fail. A successful marriage cannot be built on unrealistic expectations.

Since real love is an unconditional commitment to the good of another, the attitude that seeks to change the other partner is often based on selfish motives. Selfishness and true love are incompatible. Being committed to the good of another involves making sacrifices, giving, and yielding — all without *demanding* repayment or reward.

"Submitting Yourselves One to Another"

Ephesians 5:21, the doorway to the apostle Paul's discussion about marriage and the family, speaks of *submitting yourselves one to another in the fear of God.* Here, I believe, is the key to success in marriage. I know it works, for it has worked for Jack and me, and I've seen it work in *many* marriages. It can be summed up in a single word: submission. I am not speaking of some kind of self-abdication that makes a woman subservient to her husband, but a *mutual*, biblical submission that makes a husband and wife partners together in life.

What this means is that the husband and wife should be more concerned about the desires, the preferences, and the needs of their spouse than they are with their own. The result of such an attitude is a relationship where nothing is demanded and nothing is expected. Rather, everything is given freely and received with gratitude and humility. Instead of yearning to be served, each yearns to serve — that is real love.

You can see how this kind of love cannot be damaged by unfulfilled expectations. It asks for nothing, it insists on nothing — it just gives and sacrifices. It is not manipulative, it is not suspicious, and it takes nothing for granted. I believe that if we will strive to infuse that kind of love into our marriages, we can guarantee their success.

There is a deep satisfaction that comes with submitting ourselves one to another. Jack and I have experienced it in our marriage. In earlier days when we had very little materially, we were content just to be together. We never felt we needed money or houses or things to make our marriage better. Just enjoying each other was more than enough.

This remains true today. The Lord has blessed us in many ways, and yet our greatest enjoyment still comes from being together and enjoying each other's presence. Although we both like to "get away from it all" each year, we do not limit our vacation plans to where I want to go or what Jack would like to do. Instead, we try to determine how we can spend our time *together.* A few years ago, for example, we vacationed in Toronto. Rather than spending a lot of money on activities to keep us entertained, we took long walks together. In fact, we walked about ten miles a day, just talking, sharing, and spending time with each other. Our marriage is a partnership in which friendship, respect, affection, and the wonder of love all play key roles. We do not need external, artificial, or material things to make it work.

Taking Time to Share

The value of sharing in marriage cannot be overemphasized. The truth of the matter is that the inability of one or both partners to truly care about and become involved in the life of the other is one of the major reasons that interest and affection often begin to wane in the early years of wedlock. Instead of becoming a part of each other, husbands and wives all too frequently find themselves drifting apart.

As I have already indicated, sharing does not have to be contrived or implemented as a duty or chore. Indeed, it should be a natural outflow of the bond of oneness into which the bride and groom entered on their wedding day. Just taking the time to talk about goals, desires, decisions, accomplishments — perhaps even fears and frustrations — is all that is required. The mutual commitment of each to the other will do the rest.

One of the most beautiful aspects of my walk with Jack has been our continual ability to communicate. There has never been anything about which we could not talk. One of the most endearing compliments he has given to me was on an occasion when he arrived home from the office, walked into the kitchen, put his arm around me, and said, "The sweetest part of my day is being able to come home to you and talk about everything that has happened." We started talking on our honeymoon, and we have never stopped. I have to smile, even as I share this with you, at the number of times we have entered an elevator in a hotel talking about something, and five minutes later we realized we forgot to push the button for the floor to which we were going. Oh, there have been those times of silent communication, also.

The best gift I could give Jack, while he was memorizing God's Word in our motel room, was the gift of my silence. This silence was good for me as well, for it taught me the importance of using quiet times to my advantage — reading the Bible, praying, practicing, writing letters, composing an article for our magazine, or simply meditating. It is important to meditate and communicate with God in our thoughts. How long has it been since you enjoyed a silent time of direct communication with our heavenly Father? However, even during the quiet times, Jack and I were never far apart in communicating. Does this sound strange? You can know each other so well that even a smile, a gaze, or a nod of the head can be beautiful communication.

I also want to mention that the need for sharing increases tremendously as children are born. Then, more than ever, quality time spent together in activities that involve every family member will enrich one's life immensely. One of the most important and valuable things is a family devotional time when dad, as the head of the home, shares his faith with those whom God has entrusted to his care. A caring, concerned, loving father will never neglect the responsibility and opportunity to *Train up a child in the way he should go* (Proverbs 22:6).

From a social standpoint, family companionship does not have to cost a lot of money. There are many types of wholesome and enjoyable activities that do not cost anything. You can go to a museum, spend a day at the lake or park, attend an outdoor concert, or just go for a drive in the country. Each of these is more valuable than spending time mindlessly absorbed in a television program. And with children, just the fact that you care means more than any material possession you might give them.

Let me stress the truth that no one can have the proper kind of marriage or family relationship without a willingness to give as well as to receive. Perhaps this concept seems foreign to everything you have come to believe. Ours is a society preoccupied with rights: women's rights, children's rights, civil rights, personal rights, and every other kind of rights. Although many of these rights are important elements of a free society, they can also bring death to individual relationships and especially to marriage. Real love *demands* no rights.

One of the purest forms of human love is that of a mother for her baby. Such love is totally selfless and sacrificial. The mother feeds the child, changes him, rocks him, responds when he cries, holds him when he needs her, sings to him, and does virtually everything for him. What does she get from the child in return? Only the satisfaction of having loved. He is too small to return her love in a meaningful way. He can do nothing but demand more of her time and attention. Still, any good mother will tell you that nothing is more satisfying than caring for the needs of an infant.

My heart is deeply grieved by the *un*natural affection displayed by some mothers and fathers today. They are unhappy with themselves, but instead of facing the issue openly and honestly, they project their deep-seated dissatisfaction toward their children — even to the point of blaming them for their problems and the irritations of daily life. The result is often child abuse.

A few months ago, when Jack and I were in Brussels, we were walking in the downtown area and passed in front of an arcade. It seemed that there were hundreds of kids hanging out there, playing the machines, totally absorbed in that activity. I remember turning to Jack and saying, "I wonder what their homelife is like."

Today, in almost any town in our country, you will find the same situation, proving that family relationships are at a disturbingly low ebb in our nation. What is happening to homelife?

Jack and I were unable to have children. (I explain this in my book *The Tender Touch.*) But if we had been blessed with a family, I would have wanted it to be a closely knit family where we spent time together playing games, reading, having fun, or conducting good discussions. I would have endeavored to make our homelife so appealing and so attractive that our children would have been drawn to it, like a magnet.

I interviewed Georg Andersen, an interior designer with many years' experience in various settings, both commercial and residential. I was immediately attracted to his book *Interior Decorating: A Reflection of the Creator's Design* because of the cover. It shows a beautifully decorated room, but what caught my attention was the glass-topped coffee table with two children's chairs alongside. When I read the book I learned that this was the Andersen living room. Provision had been made for the youngest members of the family. I was impressed.

This is a subject on which I could spend a great deal of time because, even though I don't have children, it is a topic that is very dear to my heart. My mind is troubled every time I see children who look unhappy and lonely; I cry when I read stories of child abuse and hear of child abandonment.

I heard, in the course of writing this book, about a Christian young couple going through divorce — the mother had walked out of the marriage leaving behind three small children. Even though she left them with her husband, she was still walking away from her God-given role as a mother. I must confess I do not understand how any woman can do this. She was obviously dissatisfied with the marriage. To walk out on her husband is one thing, but to leave those precious children is something else. I wept when I heard this story.

I do not know the circumstances surrounding that couple's failed marriage. I do know there are some cases of wife-abuse, which would necessitate a separation. (Such was not the case in this instance, I have been assured.) We gaze in disbelief about newspaper headlines which speak of wife-beating (and now even husband-beating!), but the fact remains that such incidents are increasing steadily in our society.

We need to realize that the Bible predicts that such an attitude will be prevalent in the "last days," just prior to Christ's return (see II Timothy 3:3). If you know someone suffering under such conditions or are yourself its victim, seek help immediately. A pastor or qualified Christian counselor will be both able and happy to assist you.

True love, then, gives and keeps on giving. This is the kind of love it takes to make a marriage work — love that demands nothing and expects nothing; love that delights to serve and to meet needs; love that finds its deepest satisfaction in giving, not receiving.

Such love does not come easily. The mother who waits on her baby was once a baby herself, crying for her own needs to be fulfilled. All of us began that way, and the selfishness of our infancy is something that is not quickly conquered. It takes a great deal of wisdom and maturity to see that satisfaction comes in serving others. Then it takes a great deal of character to have the strength of will to commit oneself to a life of self-sacrifice.

Still, this emptying of self is exactly what is

required to make a marriage (or any kind of human relationship) workable, fruitful, and rewarding.

Real satisfaction is always just out of reach for those who refuse to submit, sacrifice, and serve. They can never quite obtain what they believe it would take to make them content. The message of God's Word is this: satisfaction in marriage, in the family, in business, in school, and in life itself is only for those who deny themselves and delight in serving others.

Marriage, possibly more than any other area of life, is a good gauge of our satisfaction. I do not know of anyone who has a successful marriage who is not basically satisfied. And I know of few whose marriages are failing who will say they are satisfied. Perhaps you are dissatisfied with your marriage. Have you been looking to the wrong sources for satisfaction? Have you been demanding more than giving? Maybe you are shirking rather than accepting responsibility. Will you ask God to teach you what it is to surrender completely — to Him first, and then to your spouse? I know that if you are able to learn this basic truth and apply it to your life and marriage, your discontentment will vanish and you can begin anew.

A Little Dissatisfaction May Be Good for You

All of us at one time or another have known dissatisfaction. No one enjoys being dissatisfied, but by the same token dissatisfaction is not always bad. Consider the following with me, if you will: If we were not dissatisfied we wouldn't change and we wouldn't grow. And if we didn't grow, we would atrophy.

We dare not make the mistake of thinking that satisfaction is the same thing as smugness. Smugness is a sort of self-satisfaction, and self-satisfaction is not true satisfaction. Quite the contrary, self-satisfaction breeds apathy, pride, and a holier-than-thou attitude. It is a work of the flesh, not a fruit of the Spirit.

At least one kind of dissatisfaction is both beneficial and desirable. It is revealed in Paul's words in Philippians 3:12-14:

Not as though I had already attained, either were already perfect: *but I follow after, if that I may apprehend that for which also I am apprehended of Christ Jesus. Brethren,* ***I count not myself to have apprehended:*** *but this one thing I do, forgetting those things which are behind, and reaching forth unto those things which are before, I press toward the mark for the prize of the high calling of God in Christ Jesus* (emphasis added).

In this passage, Paul was affirming that he did not feel he had arrived at a point of perfection. He was, in a sense, dissatisfied. He knew there were things he could do better. He was aware of certain areas in his life that could be improved. In other words, he had room in his life to grow.

The great apostle responded to this inner feeling of need in a beautiful way. Rather than brooding over his past failures and allowing his sense of imperfection to become an excuse for depression and self-rejection, he acknowledged and accepted them. Then, refusing to abandon himself to failure, he dedicated himself more completely to his purpose of striving to be what God wanted him to be.

We need to develop the same attitude if we are ever to be truly satisfied. We must forget our past failures and press on toward the mark. We must refuse to sink into self-pity or apathy. Above all, we must refuse to become discouraged. Real satisfaction is within reach, but it requires that we have a healthy dose of the right kind of *dis*satisfaction.

The Untidy-Home Syndrome

Few people like to do housework, but most of us recognize the need to do it. Truly how a woman keeps her home is *very important* and reveals a lot about how she views herself and what she thinks of her husband. In fact, an untidy house is often a sign of a life out of order. A heart in disarray can show itself through a home that is also in disarray. One of the first things a woman seeking to escape often does is neglect her house. She may spend the day watching soap operas, talking on the telephone, or doing something else without much meaning to escape the responsibility of housekeeping.

In this sense, I think the women's rights movement has been especially detrimental to women. Much of their rhetoric implies that being a mother and wife is not enough. It is wrong to strip those domestic tasks of their inherent dignity. Being a wife and mother is an important — yes, even a glorious — calling, and assuredly every homemaker ought to do her work with great pride and the very best she can.

There is an old motto which expresses so well the way I feel about a home. I think you will agree it says it well:

> The beauty of the house is order;
> The blessing of the house is contentment;
> The glory of the house is hospitality;
> The crown of the house is godliness.
>
> (Author unknown)

Interior designer Georg Andersen suggests we ask ourselves these five questions to check our home's "condition":

1. When my doorbell rings, does my house echo my greeting, "Welcome — come in and sit down?"

2. Does it offer a place of contentment, tranquility, edification, and sturdy affection?

3. Do my children like to bring their friends home?

4. Is it my church away from church?

5. *Does it glorify God*? [1]

He emphasizes that our homes should and can do all these things. I couldn't agree more.

Edith Schaeffer (wife of Dr. Frances Schaeffer of L'Abri — the Christian fellowship center they established in the Swiss Alps) talks much on "continuity" in life — the need to surround ourselves with 'things' that are familiar and dear. She and Dr. Schaeffer are worldwide travelers; yet, Edith always tucks a much-loved object — a candle, or a small embroidered tablecloth, something homey and familiar — into her bag when they leave home. Her book *Hidden Art* is choice reading for the woman who wishes to enrich her family's home life. She speaks much of the satisfaction that can well up in a woman's heart when she uses whatever creative gifts the Lord has given her for the beautification of her home. She challenges each woman to make the place where her family is living — regardless of its duration — a special place, a place where you express yourself. She says, "This place should communicate something of *you* to your visitors, but it should also *satisfy* something within you. You should *feel* 'at home' here because you have made it home with something of yourself."

My heart echoes these sentiments. Of course, we are limited in some respects by financial factors, and some women are more creative than others. But there is great satisfaction in making something out of nothing, in restoring something old that may have been given to you or has been rescued from someone else's discards. So many make the mistake of ignoring the present with its many possibilities, while wistfully thinking, "It will be so nice when I can afford to do this or that." *Today* is really all that we have; learn to make the most of what you have in the time you have *now.*

I believe that women who are "domestic engineers" should be just as goal-oriented as those who work outside the home. Likewise, a woman who works outside the home should approach her domestic duties with the same enthusiasm as she approaches her outside career.

Jack and I have spent a lot of time away from home over the years, and that means, of course, that we have stayed in hundreds of hotel and motel rooms. Living this life-style has never bothered me, since I felt it was a part of our calling and a small "sacrifice" I could make for the reward of being called into the Lord's service.

While on the road, people often ask me if I miss my home. Actually, I don't allow myself to think about it too much. Instead, I try to make our accommodations a "home away from home." I have always enjoyed finding little things to do to the room to make it seem better, brighter, and more homey. I will admit, however, that I always love going to our own home. We have lived in the same house for many years now, and whenever we return from a long period of time away, it always seems to welcome us.

When it comes to the household chores themselves, I enjoy putting on the happiest music I can find as I go about my duties. Music has always been an important part of our lives, and it seems to make even the most difficult tasks a delightful way to spend time. I truly enjoy making our home clean, desirable, and as lovely as possible.

Let me point you in the direction of three excellent books that might help you become a better homemaker. Each of these books speaks of the need to become aware of time and set priorities and shows you how to combat procrastination, how to set up a home filing system, how to salvage and recycle clothing, how to entertain with confidence, how to use leftover foods creatively, and how to utilize your God-given talents and abilities. Here they are: *How To Get Your Act Together (When Nobody Gave You the Script)* by Pat McBride, *More Hours in My Day* by Emilie Barnes, and *The Messies Manual (The Procrastinator's Guide to Good Housekeeping)* by Sandra Felton.

Make room in your life for reading things of this nature that can help you in some very practical ways. I am an organized person by nature, but I know many women who are not. It's nothing to be ashamed of — you have virtues that someone else doesn't possess.

But it doesn't mean that you and your family have to suffer through endless confusion. This is an area of dissatisfaction that can be conquered through some very important steps you can take immediately.

Some women, however, seem to have the kind of temperament that dislikes and detests housework. How can they change? The secret, I believe, is in being dissatisfied enough to want to change. This is where dissatisfaction can become a good emotion.

Dissatisfied Enough to Change

God often uses our dissatisfaction to make us the best that we can be. Surely when we're dissatisfied with something we become more willing to change it, more anxious to improve. God can take that yearning to be better and, through His power working in us, begin to transform us to be more and more like He wants us to be.

I have always been slim, and I even remember a time in my teenage years when I was literally gangly. Like most teenagers, I was self-conscious and not entirely satisfied with my appearance. I thought my teeth were crooked; I thought I was too skinny; and I thought *everything* was wrong with the way I looked.

One day I went to my wise and understanding mother who was always completely honest with me and with tears said, "Mother, I think I look awful." She said, "Well, you don't look your best, honey, but let's work on it." Rather than minimize my dissatisfaction, she wisely decided to use it for my benefit. First of all, she began to build up my confidence. She tried to help me see which of my features could be emphasized and which ones could be improved. She helped me realize that I could look better with a little work and determination, but she brought into focus the importance of accepting the areas that couldn't be changed. With her tender love and wisdom, she taught me that what we *are* is, after all, more important than how we look.

So many women today are dissatisfied because they, too, are frustrated with their appearance. Still, instead of doing what should and can be done about it, they allow themselves to become trapped in an attitude of self-pity and despair. Ladies, I want to encourage you to sit up, think straight, and replace your self-pity with self-determination — the determination to look, feel, and *be* your very best!

Neva Coyle has written two best-selling books on the subject of feeling better about yourself. From a defeated, discouraged housewife who didn't like how she looked or how the world was passing her by, she became a free woman. These books tell the story: *Free To Be Thin* and *Living Free*.

At one time or another, each of us needs to be encouraged to improve our appearance. (If you don't believe me, just ask your husband!) And, for those of us who are married, this is an important consideration. Our concern serves as an indication that we still care — that we want our husbands to continue to be satisfied and happy with the choice they made. Those of you who are still single need to remember that *man* [does look] *on the outward appearance* (I Samuel 16:7), and accept the validity of that portion of the verse.

May I also point out that these comments are not in contradiction to my statement in chapter 1 concerning contemporary humanity's obsession with outward appearances. Although we must not allow that which is outward to control us, we must remember that it is important. Someone has well said, "First impressions are lasting impressions," and this is so true.

The central point, then, is one of *attitude*. If we know we have done all that we should do and can do to look and be our very best, then we *are* our very best. Problems in this area arise only when we allow our dissatisfaction to overrule rather than help us to overcome the poorer aspects of our physical appearance. Perhaps the entire subject can best be summarized by the familiar quote: "Lord, grant me the grace to change the things I can, to accept the things I cannot change, and the wisdom to know the difference."

Hard work, even in the area of trying to better our appearance, is important. If we can improve ourselves by working at it, God expects us to do so. All too often we ask the Lord to give us more than we deserve, simply because we are not willing to apply ourselves.

Florence Littauer has written another very down-to-earth book that I think every woman should read. It's entitled, *It Takes So Little To Be Above Average.* The gist of her message is that we shouldn't be satisfied to be just average when it's so easily within our grasp to be above average. So whether it's dissatisfaction with your weight, your personality, your intellect, your home, your family relationships, your other relationships — set some new goals, take aim, and then go for it.

Setting goals is most essential. I learned very early in life that to succeed, a person must have goals, but above all, they must be the right kind of goals. They must be realistic and attainable. Set your personal goals so that they are within reach. Then when you accomplish them, set higher ones — a new plateau.

Recognizing Your Areas of Need

The key to growth, improvement, and maturity is this: have a realistic picture of the deficiencies in your life. Don't make excuses for your shortcomings, but do not be obsessed with them either. One attitude leads to pride, and the other leads to discouragement. Both are detrimental to your growth as a person.

I'm glad my mother did not try to convince me that there was nothing wrong with the way I looked as a teenager. By telling me honestly that I could improve myself and then helping me do it, she instilled in me a sense of self-confidence and a desire for growth. Through it, I learned to live with an accurate picture of myself, understanding both my needs and my strengths. And that is a healthy step in the right direction toward the kind of satisfaction God wants us to have.

At the beginning of this chapter, I quoted Paul's words from Philippians 3. Obviously, he never saw himself as faultless. None of us should either, for we all have shortcomings.

Most Christians tend to think of Paul as a "super saint," and truly he *was* an extremely godly man. He was disciplined, dedicated, and mightily used of God. But he was also painfully aware of his great spiritual needs. Romans 7 describes his inner struggle between the flesh and the spirit. Finally in desperation he cried out: *O wretched man that I am!* (verse 24). Paul's cry was not one of defeat, but rather the deep, heartfelt yearning of a godly man who wanted to be more godly. Far from giving up in defeat, Paul was simply using his inner dissatisfaction to spur himself on to even greater victory!

This message of determination runs throughout Paul's writings. Please notice a significant truth from his life: as he grew and matured, his sense of personal need only deepened. One would think that as a person wins new victories and attains higher goals, his sense of need would begin to diminish. Just the opposite is true. As we grow closer and closer to what God wants us to become, the more deeply we sense our shortcomings.

How beautifully illustrated this truth is in Paul's life. In one of his early writings (I Corinthians), he described himself as *least of the apostles* (15:9). What humility for one to see himself as last in order of importance and first in order of need.

Later, Paul wrote to the Ephesians, [I] *am less than the least of all saints* [or Christians] (3:8). Now he had demoted himself even further. Not only did he see himself as the least of the apostles, but he had also placed himself at the bottom of the list of all believers.

Finally, toward the end of his life, in a letter written to Timothy, Paul described himself as the chief of sinners (see I Timothy 1:15). Thus he had moved from viewing himself as a lowly apostle to seeing himself as chief among sinners. Here is a man who knew the right kind of dissatisfaction — the kind that spurred him on to greater consecration and, in my opinion, to becoming one of God's choicest servants.

I am glad for the kind of dissatisfaction that leads one to look for ways to bring about self-improvement. Like Paul, we need to cultivate this kind of dissatisfaction. We need to let it drive us to a greater dependency on the Lord. Indeed, we need to search for and cooperate with His master plan for our lives. When the work of God is complete in us and we reflect His glory, then and only then can we be completely, wholly satisfied.

Footnotes

1. Georg Andersen, *Interior Decorating* (Minneapolis, Minnesota: Bethany Publishers, 1983), p. 11.

Getting Rid of Negative Feelings

Most of us are constantly battling our negative feelings, or we are relying too heavily upon them. Everyone likes to feel good, and no one enjoys being depressed or tension ridden. Some people spend their entire lives in search of the ultimate emotional "high," while others seem to revel in feeling "low." Regardless of what kind of person you are, your feelings and how you respond to them play a major role in determining how much you can experience and enjoy satisfaction.

As we have already learned, being satisfied is not the same thing as being happy. Happiness is our emotional response to "happenings" around us and to us. Conversely, a truly satisfied person remains satisfied in grief, under pressure, and during other times of negative emotional expression. Genuine satisfaction, then, is *not* an emotion, and it is not dependent on a positive emotional response to a given situation.

Nevertheless, negative emotions, if dealt with incorrectly, can destroy satisfaction. If we see our trials as coming from God in order to bring us to maturity, for example, we can be satisfied even in the midst of deep tribulation. But if we resist trials and allow them to make us bitter, we destroy the possibility of satisfaction. This is true for every kind of negative emotion and feeling.

Bitterness, Resentment, and an Unforgiving Spirit

Quite often, negative feelings are an indication that there is something wrong in our lives. A personal failure, a broken promise, or something someone said has hurt us or undermined our sense of self-confidence. As a result, we begin brooding over the situation and harboring critical thoughts. Then, before we realize it, we find ourselves on the threshold of bitterness and resentment.

One of the most negative attitudes we as human beings can experience is an unforgiving spirit. Nothing is more damaging to a person's spiritual and emotional well-being. Yet, often, we find it so difficult to forgive.

Following a crusade several years ago, a young woman came to me in tears. "Oh, Rexella," she cried, "I can't forgive him, but after your husband's message tonight I can at least say that I'm on the road to forgiveness and I no longer hate him." She then related to me one of the saddest stories I have ever heard.

As a young child, this woman had been left alone and put up for adoption. After many years of struggling to organize her life into one that had meaning and purpose, she was adopted by a Christian family. As a teenager, she had accepted Jesus Christ as her Saviour. Later, she married a fine Christian man, and God blessed them with three beautiful children. Her life was full and complete.

The couple enjoyed the friendship of many Christians in their local church. One young man seemed especially precious to them, and they frequently invited him into their home. He evidenced a pleasant manner, and they appreciated knowing one of like faith who appeared to be living consistently for Christ.

But one afternoon the young mother returned home to find her 10-year-old daughter in tears. The young man they had loved and trusted had sexually assaulted her!

Although that had occurred two years in the past, the trauma of the experience was still very real in the life of this mother. She wept as she told me how she had for two years nurtured hatred and bitterness against the man that assaulted her daughter, and now because of it, her life was in chaos.

As I listened, I could not keep back my tears. I shared that woman's anger over what had happened to her young daughter. Together we wept over the child, the crime, and the entire situation. The words choked in my throat as I tried to help her find the strength to forgive this man for his evil deed. God had already given her the grace to stop hating this man, and now He could give her the grace to forgive him. I assured her that God shared her hatred for the evil done to her daughter, for Scripture assures us that He cares for children in a special way (see Matthew 18:6). I also showed her from the Word of God that we cannot believe everyone who says he knows Christ. Finally, I emphasized that she *must* forgive this man for his sin against her family, just as God had forgiven her when as a teenager she accepted His forgiveness for her sin against Him.

We prayed, read the Word, talked, and prayed some more. At the end of our time together, the woman was radiant — at peace with the Lord and at peace with herself. She had forgiven that man, but she was the one who benefited most from the act of forgiveness.

Most of us will never know from what depths of God's resources this woman had to draw in order to forgive. The crime committed against her daughter was unspeakable, and she had carried that memory with her for two years. But the bitterness that grew inside her because she would not forgive had begun to destroy her, and she could not be satisfied until she was released from the bondage of an unforgiving spirit.

That incident left an indelible mark on my memory, for it brought clearly into focus the truth that *forgiveness is always costly.* The awfulness of the sin committed against that woman and her daughter is appalling. I cannot get away from a sense of disgust and righteous indignation over a man's assaulting a young girl. And yet the greatest wrong of all in that whole situation was the wrong the mother did to herself physically, mentally, emotionally, and spiritually by refusing to forgive.

On one occasion in the life of the Lord Jesus, Peter came to Him and asked, *Lord, how oft shall my brother sin against me, and I forgive him? till seven times?* [Jesus answered,] *I say not unto thee, Until seven times: but, Until seventy times seven* (Matthew 18:21,22).

The Saviour was saying that there can be no limit to the number of times or the depth of forgiveness with which we are to forgive. None of us has a right to withhold forgiveness from another. We are not left with an option of *whether* to forgive. Jesus went on to emphasize this truth in a parable, telling of a man who had been forgiven of a massive debt but was unwilling to write off a debt of a few dollars someone owed to him. The foolishness of that man's stubbornness shows just why we must forgive: because God has forgiven us of so much.

Forgiving a person for a wrong committed against us *is* costly. It may cost us our pride, it may cost us money, or it may cost us in terms of violated rights. But God's forgiveness of us cost even more — it cost His Son. Jesus died to pay the price for our forgiveness, and in that dreadful moment that surpassed time and eternity as He hung on the cross bearing our sin, God the Father had to forsake His only begotten Son. It was an incredible price to pay to forgive undeserving sinners.

So often we hear people say, "I'll forgive him if he makes it right." That is not real forgiveness, for it requires the one who did the wrong to make it right. God does not require that of us. He forgives us continually, without reservation.

Forgiving and Forgetting

Sincere, effective forgiveness also includes another important element— forgetting. In her book, *It Feels Good to Forgive,* my friend Helen Hosier has penned an irreversible truth: "Regardless of how many times you may say to someone who has wronged you, 'I forgive you,' if you have not *forgotten* then you have failed in forgiveness. If you find it necessary to remind that individual of his or her betrayal, unfaithfulness, or untrustworthiness, then you have not truly forgiven the other person."

Forgiving and forgetting is truly God's way, for this is exactly what He does for us when we come to Him through Christ: *This is the covenant that I will make with them after those days, saith the Lord, I will put my laws into their hearts, and in their minds will I write them; And their sins and iniquities will I remember no more* (Hebrews 10:16-17). If God can forgive and forget our terrible iniquities which sent His Son to the cross, surely we cannot do less. In fact, He will give us the power to accomplish this task, for we *can do all things through Christ* who strengthens us (Philippians 4:13).

Many times our bitterness and resentment become so imbedded within us that we actually extend our anger beyond the person or situation which has hurt us and begin blaming God. Even Christians are prone to ask, "God, where were You? Why did You let it happen? I thought You loved me. What about Your promise of guidance and protection in Psalm 121?"

Erwin W. Lutzer, the pastor of Moody Church in Chicago, has a most enlightening answer for such inquiries. In his book, *Living With Your Passions,* he states: "God's love does not prevent us from the tragedies of sexual abuse or any other kind of mistreatment. Christ was God's 'beloved Son,' yet the Father didn't shield Him from the torture of the crucifixion. That crime, despite its horror, has become for us a fountain of blessing. The horror of Good Friday must be understood in the light of the joy of Easter Sunday. God can do the same with the ugly hurts of life."

Dr. Lutzer then admonishes his readers to confess their bitterness toward God. "Concentrate on His infinite grace and be forgiven and accepted," he says. Only in this way will you be able to experience the deep spiritual release and sense of relief which are the beginning of true satisfaction.

How to Have Right Attitudes

Perhaps you are struggling with bitterness or an unforgiving spirit and wonder how you can ever come to the point of confession, forgiveness, and being set free. Let me share with you the secret to removing wrong attitudes and negative feelings. It is the power of the Word of God.

Hebrews 4:12 says: *For the word of God is quick, and powerful, and sharper than any two edged sword, piercing even to the dividing asunder of soul and spirit, and of the joints and marrow, and is a discerner of the thoughts and intents of the heart.* In other words, when you let Scripture fill your heart, it transforms what is in there. It seeks out wrong attitudes, exposes them, and then makes them right.

The best way to let Scripture do that is to get to know

it better. Read it every day, memorize it, and meditate on it. James 1:21 speaks of *the engrafted word, which is able to save your souls.* When Scripture gets into your life and becomes a living part of you, it has an incredible transforming power.

Peter wrote something very similar: *Wherefore laying aside all malice, and all guile, and hypocrisies, and envies, and all evil speakings, As newborn babes, desire the sincere milk of the word, that ye may grow thereby* (I Peter 2:1,2). Again, Scripture is the antidote to wrong attitudes.

I am convinced that one of the reasons my husband has been so blessed of God in the ministry is that early in life he comitted himself to memorizing Scripture. Now he knows thousands of Bible verses by heart and is called, "The Walking Bible." I am often asked what it is like to live with a man who has memorized so much Scripture. My answer is, "It is wonderful." God's Word is constantly working in Jack's heart to guide him, mold him, shape his attitudes, and direct his life.

All this victory is the result of Jack's tremendous desire, determination, and discipline — and it is an ongoing process. He continues to add to his storehouse of memory verses each month. The most wonderful, miraculous thing about Scripture is that the more we appropriate it, the greater our appetite for it becomes.

Through the years, God's Word has changed Jack's personality from that of a teenage practical joker to the mature man he is today. He still has his sense of humor and enjoys a good time, but he also exhibits a seasoned wisdom that comes only from an intimate knowledge of God's Word. My life has been immeasurably enriched by living with this godly man for whom the Bible is his meat and drink. Jack has not only memorized the Word, but he also puts it into practice daily.

This is the essential element in building right attitudes — a willing and submissive obedience to the teaching of God's Word. James says we should be doers of the Word and not hearers only, deceiving our own selves. Knowing the Bible intellectually without practicing it experientially can actually harden us to its truth!

God's ideal for you is a life of victory over negative feelings. He wants you to cut out all roots of bitterness, regardless of how painful the cutting process may be. He also wants you to receive the engrafted Word, which is able to transform your soul. This is where we begin to reach the pinnacle of satisfaction.

Some time ago, I received a wonderful little note from Mrs. Howard Graves of Holland, Michigan. She wrote, "Through your ministry this week, the Lord revealed areas of my life where my supersensitivity has robbed me of victory. I seem never to learn fully that people can never hurt us unless we permit them to do so." With that note she sent this little poem that she had written several years earlier:

> I've asked the Lord to take from me
> The supersensitivity
> That robs the soul of joy and peace
> And causes fellowship to cease;
> The things that people do and say

To foster hurt along the way.
I trust that by His Spirit sweet
I may those very people meet,
And show them that His love in me
Has won another victory.

The dart which carelessly they threw
Much closer to the Saviour drew
This heart, inclined to feel the pain
Of idle words they spoke in vain.
I asked Him why it hurt so much
When they upon my life should touch;
Then quickly He revealed to me
My supersensitivity.
"Just leave it here," He seemed to say,
"The victory can be yours today.

"Remember that each idle word
My listening ear has also heard.
Before you brought that hurt to me
My eyes the one who spoke did see.
The victory is yours today
If you will put that hurt away,
Remembering that love will grow
If only you will show it." So,
I've asked the Lord to take from me
All supersensitivity.

Nell Rose Graves

Thank you, Nell, for sharing the wonderful insight the Lord has given you. May the words of your poem be my readers' prayer, today and always.

Supreme Satisfaction

I want to let you in on the greatest truth I know. Everything I can say about real satisfaction is centered in this fact. Without it, none of us can ever be genuinely satisfied.

This truth has transformed millions of people throughout the history of the world. It has made derelicts into saints, hypocrites into godly men and women, and sinners into children of God. It is the truth of salvation in Jesus Christ.

Throughout this book, we have touched on some priceless spiritual verities that have a direct bearing on whether or not we are satisfied. In fact, we might say that genuine satisfaction is completely a spiritual issue. To me, satisfaction is the normal state of a healthy soul. A person who neglects his spiritual needs cuts himself off from the possibility of knowing real and lasting satisfaction.

The greatest spiritual truth of all is what God has done to redeem us from our sin. By giving His Son to die in our place, God has paid the price of our sin and is able to save us from the bondage and dissatisfaction that comes with it.

Let me clearly say that I am not speaking of religion. Many people who are religious know nothing about salvation. Religion is of human origin, and it almost always requires that we *do* something. God's salvation, however, is entirely His work on our behalf. It requires absolutely nothing, since God has already accomplished all that is necessary on our behalf. Our part is that we simply accept it by faith.

A Personal Commitment

I have been privileged to conduct two wonderful interviews with the Reverend Peter Marshall. He grew up in a marvelous Christian family. His father, the late Dr. Peter Marshall, was for many years chaplain of the United States Senate, and his mother, the late Catherine Marshall, is known and loved by millions for the many wonderful books she has written.

I asked Peter what impact his distinguished parents had on his coming to Christ. He explained that they had made clear to him from his youth just what it means to be a Christian. As a result, he never took Christianity for granted, and he never assumed that just because his parents were well-known Christian leaders, he was automatically a Christian as well.

In fact, Peter told me it was not until he was

21 years of age that he felt he had really committed his life to the Lord. Although he had grown up surrounded by Christian teaching and in his head knew it was true, he had not yielded his heart in making a personal commitment to Jesus Christ.

"I graduated from college, and I was lost," he told me. "I had no idea who I was or why I was here. I thought I was going into the foreign service, the United States Diplomatic Corps, but the Lord shut that door, and that didn't work out. So I had nothing. No plans. No Goals. Nothing.

"Then I went to a Fellowship of Christian Athletes conference in Colorado in the summer of 1961 and heard Don Moomaw speak. I gave my life to the Lord as a result of that encounter. Two weeks later I was in seminary, and in 1965 I was ordained to the gospel ministry."

God took Peter Marshall's aimless life and gave him direction. And, as I interviewed him, Peter expressed his concern and burden that many people do not understand what Christianity really is.

"Christianity is not just running around trying to do great things for God," he said. "We must understand that we need Jesus Christ because we are sinful human beings — weak and needy. In my pride, I had a hard time accepting this."

I believe one of the reasons so many people — so many *religious* people — are dissatisfied is that they perceive religion as something *we* do for God. But true satisfaction begins when we accept what *God* has done for us! The Bible says, *For by grace are ye saved through faith; and that not of yourselves: it is the gift of God: Not of works, lest any man should boast* (Ephesians 2:8,9).

You see, if salvation were something we could earn for ourselves, it would only contribute to our pride, for when we earned salvation, we would have much about which to brag and boast. Thus, what Peter Marshall says is absolutely correct — all of us are needy sinners: *There is none righteous, no, not one . . . . For all have sinned, and come short of the glory of God* (Romans 3:10,23). Yes, all of us fall short of God's standards, and if we are to receive salvation from our sins, we must receive it as a gift, not as a meritorious award for service.

What Sin Does to Us

Some may have difficulty accepting the fact that all of us are sinners. We all know people who are good, moral, honest, generous, thoughtful human beings. Surely they are not sinners in the same way hardened criminals are sinners — are they?

From God's perspective, the answer is "yes." Because His standard is absolute holiness — one hundred precent perfection — the issue is not how many sins we commit or what kind of sins we commit, but *if we have sinned at all.* And Scripture is clear that none of us can honestly say we have never sinned.

In the presence of absolute holiness, even the smallest sin is as offensive and out of place as the darkest, most heinous act of evil one can imagine. Because God is so completely holy and uncompromisingly righteous, He cannot permit sin to exist in His presence. And the only equitable penalty for sin is death:

For the wages of sin is death (Romans 6:23).

But just as God is holy, righteous, and just, Scripture also informs us that He is a God of love. And because of His great love for us, He does not wish to condemn us without mercy. Since in His righteousness He cannot simply overlook sin, He found a way that He could make us righteous without compromising His own holiness. However, it cost Him the sacrifice of His Son!

Perhaps the most familiar verse in all of Scripture is John 3:16: *For God so loved the world, that he gave his only begotten Son, that whosoever believeth in him should not perish, but have everlasting life.* That verse, more than any other, has opened people's eyes to the truth of God's salvation and the way to real satisfaction.

Salvation Explained

What this all means is that you do not have to earn God's approval. You do not have to work to make yourself righteous. You do not have to become deserving of God's grace. All the work has been done by God himself, and He offers His grace freely to those who will receive it by faith!

Nothing gives a greater sense of personal worth than the truth that God loves us so much that He gave His Son to pay the price for our sins. And nothing on earth brings more complete satisfaction than the confidence of knowing you are secure in God's salvation.

May I ask you some important personal questions? What are you counting on to make yourself acceptable to God? If you were to stand before Him and give an account of your life, what could you point to that might make you acceptable to Him? Would it be your own works of righteousness? I hope not, because Isaiah 64:6 says: *. . . all our righteousnesses are as filthy rags.* God cannot accept works of "righteousness" from unrighteous people. Would you point to your heritage? Scripture is clear that salvation is not anyone's birthright. In fact, Jesus said, *Except a man be born again, he cannot see the kingdom of God* (John 3:3).

The only thing any of us can point to that makes us acceptable to God is the work of Jesus Christ on our behalf. We must simply trust Him with childlike faith and receive His gift of eternal life (Romans 6:23).

Be Sure

I was privileged to grow up in a Christian home. My parents, two brothers (Bob and Don), and I attended a fine church, and Christianity was our way of life. By the age of 6, I was singing in church and even introducing my own songs. I felt good about performing in church services and about almost everything in my life during those early years.

As a little girl, I was impressed with the importance of telling others about Jesus. In grade school, I received permission to read a Bible story to my class each day. When I reached junior high, I witnessed to my classmates often and invited many of them to the services and activities of my church.

Entering high school, I maintained a positive outward witness because I loved this way of life. Still, deep within, I began to sense that all was not well in my relationship with God. Sometimes during those years serious doubts about my salvation entered my mind. Usually, however, I brushed them aside as groundless. After all, I had known about the Lord all my life, and a great part of my time was occupied in church activities.

The moment of truth came during a Sunday evening service at our church. I was 16, and the soloist for that very service. My pastor spoke with his usual earnestness, and although following my solo I had taken a seat in the rear of the auditorium, I was well within reach of the convicting power of the Holy Spirit.

Before the pastor had finished his message, I was aware of my need to trust Christ as my personal Saviour. Unable to retain my composure, I left the auditorium and headed for my parents' car to be alone. Concerned, my father followed me and asked what was wrong.

"Oh, Dad," I sobbed, "I've deceived my own heart. I've deceived the pastor and you and our whole church. I have known *about* the Lord all my life, but I don't really *know Him.*"

It was a difficult and emotional moment for my father — and he handled it wisely. Resisting the temptation to soothe my feelings, he tenderly advised, "Be sure, Rexella."

A few weeks later, my older brother (whom I had always admired and respected for his consistent Christian life) learned of my soul's distress when he heard me crying in my room. He knelt beside me and with genuine love and compassion led me through God's plan of salvation. Although I had known all these facts for years, I had never *applied* them. Now I knew I could not wait any longer. There in my room I lost all of my religion and took Jesus Christ as my personal Saviour and Lord. At last I was *sure* of my salvation.

What a tremendous sense of freedom and satisfaction filled my soul! Joy and peace became my daily experience, and since that day I have never been uncertain about my standing before God. Since He has forgiven me and paid the price for my sins with the blood of His own Son, I know I have nothing to fear. When I sing, it is for His glory and not for the praise of men. His grace and love to me are more satisfying than money, prestige, or human recognition could ever be.

The Great Transition

In closing this chapter, may I take God's promise of complete and continuing satisfaction to its ultimate conclusion? Through a personal example, I wish to share with you the depth of the riches reserved for all who are in Christ Jesus.

One of the most powerful promises of the Bible is that, once you have become God's child, He will never leave you or forsake you (see Hebrews 13:5). Jesus himself said in John 6:37: . . . *him that cometh to me I will in no wise* [for any reason] *cast out.* And at no time during one's life will the knowledge and comfort of this blessed promise be more satisfying and assuring than at the hour through which each of us must one day pass — the hour of death.

As I have already shared in chapter 2, I approached this hour at an intersection in Brussels, Belgium, in 1979. I know what it is like to face death and then be spared by the omnipotent hand of God. I have also seen, from a human perspective, the completion of this transition in the life of a child of God who was very near and dear to me — my beloved father, Rex Shelton. Therefore, I can tell you truthfully and experiencially that there is no greater satisfaction — both for the one who is passing and those who are left behind — than to know that when a believer's life on earth ends, he is immediately ushered into the presence of Jesus for all eternity.

"Go on, Dad. We know you want to go. Go on, Dad." These words of love, understanding, and comfort were spoken by my brother Bob as our father was drawing his last breath of mortal life. My two brothers, their darling wives, and my precious husband and I had gathered at my mother's side from all parts of the country. She had not called one of us. Through the drawing power of God's Spirit, we had sensed that Dad was ready to leave us, and we all wanted to be there.

How we praise the Lord for those closing days and hours with him. We talked together, laughed together, cried together, prayed together, and loved together. The very presence of God was in that hospital room each day and night, and we experienced the serenity that He alone can give. Oh, how great is our dear Lord to condescend to care for our feelings, frustrations, and passions.

I had felt so helpless as I watched my father suffer. We had prayed for a miracle — for the healing of his body. But, as the Lord said "no" to Paul when he three times prayed to be healed of his infirmity, so God had said "no" to us. Instead, He promised a special reward and crown for Dad's patience and suffering during those 11 months of intense pain. Through it all, Dad never doubted God's love, infinite wisdom, and plan for his life. He knew Jesus was walking with him every moment and that he was not bearing the pain alone.

"Rexella, look up there." I had leaned very close to my father's side as he pointed to the wall from his bed.

"What is it, Daddy?"

"I'm walking through the valley of the shadow of death."

With all the compassion and love I had within me, I placed my hand on his and asked, "Who is waiting for you on the other side?"

Great peace shone on his face and tears welled up into his eyes as he replied, "My Lord . . . my Lord is waiting."

The valley of the shadow of death is not hurtful or painful for a believer. Just as it causes no pain to drive through the shadow of a truck on the highway, so passing through the shadow of death brings but a temporary lack of full light and brightness as we approach heaven — where Jesus himself is our light.

Just hours before Dad left us, he was still in perfect control. In fact, his departing thoughts and statements have implanted themselves into our hearts forever. He prayed over us and shared one final time his joy in knowing that we were all there to strengthen one another in family communion and love.

Finally, the doctor with whom my father had

shared his faith and the love of God for seven years informed us that Dad would be gone before the day ended. The nurses who had tenderly cared for him placed a soft, white lambskin under his body to ease the excruciating pain and through tears expressed their sorrow at losing him. They knew Dad well on that floor of the hospital and had come to love him.

As we sat around Dad, praying, remembering him, loving him, and clinging to the Lord and each other for strength, I looked up and beheld my father resting on that lambskin. "Oh, look at Daddy," I exclaimed. "How symbolic of what is occurring. He is resting on the Lamb!"

At 4 p.m., Tuesday, November 24, 1981, Dad left us for the home he had reserved as just a young boy. He had opened his heart to Jesus Christ in an evangelistic meeting and never doubted his eternal destiny thereafter.

Dad's departure into eternity, infinity, and the presence of the Lord was profound and sacred to each of us as my mother, my brothers, and I held his hands and touched his face one last time. How privileged I was to personally witness the faith, strength, and tranquility God supplies to His children when they pass through the valley of the shadow of death. How satisfying it is for me to know that one day very soon — perhaps today — I will see Dad again. He was the one who had taught me how to live, and he so beautifully taught me how to die.

At this moment, I have a deep longing in my heart. It is the longing that through the example of my precious father and the eternal truth of God's Word, you, too, will learn how to live. Then, when the hour of your homegoing has come, you will assuredly be able to say with the apostle Paul, *For to me to live is Christ, and to die is gain* (Philippians 1:21).

Oh, To Be Like Thee!

Throughout this book I have hinted at an idea that is foundational to true satisfaction. It is this: Nothing is satisfying apart from the process of being transformed into the image of God.

The ultimate satisfaction comes from developing a character that reflects the character of God. We have touched on this truth in virtually every chapter. We have seen, for example, that satisfaction comes in having a proper self-image, and now we have come full-circle — being transformed into *God's* image.

The words of Psalm 17:15 capture the essence of true satisfaction: *I shall be satisfied, when I awake, with thy likeness.* Clearly, there is no satisfaction apart from being transformed into the likeness of God. Every man has a built-in longing to be like his Creator. Not everyone identifies it as such, but just the same it is there in the deepest recesses of every person's heart. It is this yearning to be like God that proves we are human.

You see, God originally formed man in His image. When He breathed into Adam the breath of life, He was fashioning him in the likeness of Himself. At his creation, man was not tainted by sin. He was morally pure, spiritually complete and capable of intimate fellowship with his Maker. Therefore, God placed him in a perfect surrounding, provided for his every need, and walked and talked with him daily in the garden. In other words, God created man to be totally satisfied and gave him everything he needed to ensure that his satisfaction was complete.

This perfect satisfaction was lost, however, because man disobeyed God and sinned. (Talk about free will — we are not robots!) When sin entered the universe, along with it came disease, darkness, death, and all the things that contribute to mankind's dissatisfaction. Worst of all, the image of God in man was marred. Man was no longer morally pure. He could not enjoy unhindered fellowship with God. Instead, he stood guilty and condemned before God.

From that point at the very beginning of mankind's history until now, all men have sensed an inner dissatisfaction, a need for something that would truly satisfy. Each of us knows that longing for something deeply fulfilling. Indeed, it grows out of an inbred desire to know God, to fellowship with Him, and, most of all, to be like Him.

The Wrong Way to Be Like God

Recently, I interviewed Rabi Maharaj, a fascinating man with an incredible story. Rabi was studying to be a Hindu guru when God miraculously turned his life around. My interview with him was one of the most intriguing I have ever conducted.

According to Hindu beliefs, a guru is essentially a god. The word *guru* itself means "divine master." Thus, Rabi Maharaj was viewed by thousands of Hindus as a saviour. They worshipped him. They bowed to him. They prayed to him. They hung on to his every word. For them, his goal as a god was as good as achieved.

Rabi told me that he tried hard to believe that he was a god. He followed Hindu teachings strictly, and he did all that he could to live up to his image of deity. Yet, despite all these things, an emptiness gnawed at his heart.

While he was approaching the ultimate status in his religious life, Rabi had some fantastic experiences. He saw visions and entered euphoric trances. His mind was often unleashed, and he felt omniscient. He had out-of-the-body experiences during which it seemed his spirit left his body and traveled freely. He saw bright lights and mystical beings. But somehow these things did not seem right. In fact, while Rabi was studying in London, he met students who had taken LSD and other drugs. Amazingly, he discovered that their experiences had been exactly the same as his! This led him to conclude that his religion surely was not of divine origin.

Through many avenues of personally hearing God's plan of salvation, Rabi left the Hindu religion, embracing Jesus Christ as his Saviour, and his entire life was transformed. The thrilling account of his conversion is contained in his book, *The Death of A Guru*.

Those who had once worshipped Rabi now spat in his face, threw stones at him, and persecuted him. Their actions, however, did not bother him because he had found something to fill the inner void that had troubled him. For the first time in his life, he told me, he knew real satisfaction.

You see, Rabi Maharaj had tried the wrong way to be like God. Declaring oneself to be a god, trying to usurp God's authority and position, or just trying to be lord of one's own life are all the wrong approaches to seeking satisfaction. Because they are self-centered and based on human effort, they are doomed to failure. The Bible tells us that Satan also tried to be like God. Originally created as an archangel, he was privileged to see and experience God's glory daily. But for him, this was not enough. Satan, called Lucifer (Isaiah 14:12), was caught up with his high position and began to think that he could overthrow God. Rather than observe and protect God's glory, he desired it for himself. He wanted God's authority and dominion. He coveted the very throne of heaven. So God cast him out.

Satan tempted Eve with the same desire that had led to his own fall. He told her that she and Adam would be like gods if they ate the forbidden fruit. She ate it and gave it to Adam who also disobeyed, and their actions led to the fall of mankind.

Satan uses that same temptation against people today. The reason it is so effective is that it is so subtle, so close to the truth. Our desire to be like God is at least partly right. God *wants* us to be like Him.

He doesn't want us to overthrow His authority or try to steal His glory, but He does want us to share His values, His character, and His moral nature. That is why He created us — to bring glory to Him. We seriously err, however, when in our attempt to be like God, we make ourselves little gods, worshipping ourselves and demanding that others worship us. In doing so, we corrupt God's purpose in us.

God's Purpose Has Not Changed

God still wants us to be formed in His image. He has not changed His plan for mankind. This is an exciting, wonderful truth! But the transformation can only be accomplished through God's Son Jesus Christ, whom He gave to redeem the world. This is why Jesus died. Through His death by the shedding of His blood, Jesus paid the penalty for man's sin. As a result, God can redeem those who trust Christ. When one accepts Christ, he becomes a partaker of God's divine nature (see II Peter 1:4), and the process of restoration to His image has begun.

Specifically, at salvation, God transforms us and conforms us to the image of His Son (see Romans 8:29). The apostle John wrote: *. . . it doth not yet appear what we shall be: but we know that, when he shall appear, we shall be like him; for we shall see him as he is* (I John 3:2).

I interviewed the parents of Chet Bitterman, the missionary who was martyred a few years ago after being kidnapped by a group of terrorists in Bogota, Colombia. Theirs is a beautiful testimony, and the wonderful thing is that although their son gave his life in the Lord's service doing exactly what God had called him to do, Chester and Mary Bitterman are not at all angry that God permitted Chet to be killed.

Chet's father told me that his son had given his life willingly, just as they had given him willingly to the Lord. Chet, they said, was following the example of Christ by laying down his life for those he loved. They feel a tremendous loss, of course, but they are gladdened by the knowledge that Chet is now with the Lord. Truly, he followed in Christ's footsteps.

There is a great amount of satisfaction in being like Jesus, even in suffering. Paul wrote that he was willing to give up everything in order that he might *know him, and the power of his resurrection, and the fellowship of his sufferings, being made conformable unto his death* (Philippians 3:10).

You Are What You Worship

A phrase often used to encourage a healthy diet is, "You are what you eat." May I suggest a parallel to that? "You are what you worship." Yes, we become exactly like whatever or whomever we worship. The person who worships material things loses his ability to relate to that which is eternal. One who worships people becomes like those he glorifies, and one who worships false gods and images becomes identical to them!

Nowhere is this principle more clear than in Psalm 135:15-18:

> *The idols of the heathen are silver and gold, the work of men's hands.*
> *They have mouths, but they speak not; eyes have they, but they see not;*
> *They have ears, but they hear not; neither is there any breath in their mouths.*
> ***They that make them are like unto them: so is every one that trusteth in them*** [emphasis added].

This is why God forbids idol worship: it robs Him of His glory and is always unfulfilling to the worshipper himself. Those who worship wrongly can never know the satisfaction of sharing the image of God. Human religion inevitably leads to dissatisfaction. Rabi Maharaj is a testimony to this fact.

Real satisfaction, then, comes through seeing God in His glory and being remade into His likeness. Second Corinthians 3:18 says: *But we all, with open face beholding as in a glass the glory of the Lord, are changed into the same image from glory to glory.* In other words, as we worship God and behold His glory, the effect is that we are transformed by and into that glory. And as we continue learning of Him and serving Him, we move from one level of glory to another until we become like Him.

Real Satisfaction

The deepest kind of satisfaction any of us can ever know comes from living in the Lord's presence and allowing Him to change us so that we learn to think as He thinks, act as He acts, and see as He sees — with compassion and love. Nothing in all the human experience can take the place of such a relationship because it is the purpose for which God created us. Best of all, this wonderful, eternal relationship can be yours today — this very moment.

In Revelation 3:20, Christ states: *Behold, I stand at the door, and knock: if any man hear my voice, and open the door, I will come in to him, and will sup with him, and he with me.* Do you sense the Saviour tenderly knocking at the door of your heart? Will you open the door and bid Him enter? Do you believe His promise? If so, He will enter.

There is a precious little prayer that millions, down through the years, have prayed. It's called, "The Sinner's Prayer," and I want to share it with you:

The Sinner's Prayer

> *Dear Lord Jesus, I come to You just as I am, a sinner. I willingly turn from my self, sin, and unbelief to You. By faith, I trust You to save me through Your shed blood and to guide me in the Christian life. I will live for You. Amen.*

Please take a few moments to reflect on the words of this prayer. Are they an expression of the faith in your heart? Simply repeating a prayer by itself does not save, but . . . *with the heart man believeth unto righteousness; and with the mouth confession is made unto salvation* (Romans 10:10).

Christ is waiting . . . and the decision is yours. If you will receive Him, you may be assured that He will receive you, for, *These things have I written unto you . . . that ye may* ***know*** *that ye have eternal life* (I John 5:13).

Epilogue

"Parting Thoughts From My Heart"

I wish I could convey to you the peace I feel as I conclude this work. I know that my task is finished, and my mission completed. I have shared with you the deepest desires of my heart from the eternal truth of God's Word. I hope you have found my message meaningful and that it has accomplished something special in your life.

In parting, I would like to leave three brief, final thoughts with you. The first is that satisfaction should *never be considered an end in itself.* We must never seek the gift, but always the Giver. Remember: God graciously grants us success, security, and satisfaction, not because we deserve them, but because it is His nature to be a loving benefactor to His own.

Second, I would encourage you to *seek God's*

perfect will for your life. Once you have found true satisfaction, don't ever allow yourself to be drawn back toward that state of mind and life from which God has rescued you. Instead, *Trust in the Lord with all thine heart; and lean not unto thine own understanding. In all thy ways acknowledge him, and he shall direct thy paths* (Proverbs 3:5,6). God's plan and purpose for you is the highest pursuit to which you can ever commit yourself.

Finally, *never settle for second best.* It is not always easy to see *how* God works through circumstances to bring about His perfect will in our lives, but we can be assured that He does. Romans 8:28 plainly says so. And, if there is anything I have learned and relearned through all our years of ministry, it is that God can be trusted completely and without reservation. Seek Him, trust Him, and serve Him and He will not allow you to fail or lack in any way.

My fondest wish as I leave you is that, even though we have not been able to speak face-to-face, the truths which I have endeavored to impart will have touched a tender spot in your heart and mind. Indeed, I trust that you have accepted them and experienced the peace of God which passes all understanding (see Philippians 4:7).

If you have, my heart rejoices. I hope that you'll write and tell me so.

If you have not, I want to encourage you to continue considering the experiences and truths I have shared. I'll be praying and resting in the fact that our wonderful Lord is longsuffering, not willing that any should perish (see II Peter 3:9). I know He will continue working through the circumstances of your life to draw you to Himself.